P9-EMO-908

THE CHRISTIAN ISLAND

By the same author:

Poems:

DEVOURING ZODIAC

THE CHOICE

PHOENIX AND UNICORN

AIR JOURNEY

Translations:

OVID ON LOVE

THE POEMS OF FRANÇOIS VILLON (*Everyman's Library*)

SAPPHO OF LESBOS

Prose:

ARTHUR: ROMAN BRITAIN'S LAST CHAMPION (*David & Charles*)

THE CHRISTIAN ISLAND

BERAM
SAKLATVALA

WITH EIGHT PAGES
OF PLATES

LONDON
J. M. DENT & SONS LTD

Made in Great Britain
at the
Aldine Press · Letchworth · Herts
for
J. M. DENT & SONS LTD
Aldine House · Bedford Street · London
First published 1969

SBN: 460 03406 5

CONTENTS

Introduction ix

PART I. EARLY LINKS AND LEGENDS: THE FIRST AND SECOND CENTURIES

1. The Roman Conquest 3
2. Pomponia Graecina 6
3. The Cirencester Word Square 11
4. Glastonbury 14
5. King Lucius 17

PART II. CHURCH AND STATE TO THE THIRD CENTURY

1. Nero to Septimius Severus 23
2. Alexander Severus to Decius 27

PART III. THE FOURTH CENTURY

1. The First British Martyrs 33
2. Constantine: The Beginnings 36
3. The Vision of Constantine 39
4. The Edict of Milan and the Synod of Arles 41
5. Churches in Britain 45
6. Christian Villas 50
7. Other Christian Objects 54
8. The Setback 60
9. Maximus 64
10. A Christian Governor 66

PART IV. THE FIFTH CENTURY

1. Slave and Priest 71
2. North of the Wall 76

3. A British Heretic 85
4. A Christian Writer 88
5. The Soldier Bishop 90
6. A Saint in Wales 98
7. The Coming of the Pagans 99

PART V. THE SIXTH CENTURY
1. The Growing Darkness 109
2. The Enduring Faith 116
3. The Holy Isle 120
4. The Heathen Kingdoms 121
5. The Growing Isolation 126
6. The Planning of a Mission 129
7. Rome Returns 132
8. The Two Churches 138
Index 145

ILLUSTRATIONS

facing page

Coin of the Emperor Constantine the Great (*British Museum*)
Coin portrait of Helena (*British Museum*) 84

Silver spoons from the Mildenhall Treasure (*British Museum*) 85

Pewter chalice-like object from Ampleforth (*British Museum*)
Pewter bowl from Ampleforth (*British Museum*)
Pewter ingot with Chi-Rho monogram (*British Museum*) 100

Stones from Kirkmadrine, Wigtownshire (*The National Museum of Antiquities of Scotland*) 101

The Cirencester Word Square (*The Corinium Museum, Cirencester; courtesy Professor Frere*) 116

The Icklingham 'Font' (*British Museum*) 117

The Hinton St Mary mosaic (*British Museum*) 136

Wall painting, Lullingstone Villa (*Ministry of Public Building and Works*) 137

INTRODUCTION

NEARLY four hundred years after the Romans first occupied Britain their power decayed, and by about the year 400 the last of their armies left the island. With the shield of Rome's power gone, the province suffered invasion after invasion from the barbarians in the north and from the heathen tribes of Germany. Chief among the latter were the Saxons, long famous for their ferocity and their skill at sea, together with their neighbours the Angles. There followed a hundred and fifty years of bitter struggle; finally the Britons, highly civilized after their long contact with Rome, and very largely Christian, were overwhelmed and the pagan Angles and Saxons set up their warlike kingdoms in the old province. In Rome itself, memory of the island faded and Britain was again seen as a legendary and mysterious land, hidden in the long darkness of the northern seas.

Rome, no longer a great military power, but now the head and centre of the Christian world, sent St Augustine in A.D. 597 to bring the faith to the inhabitants of the now heathen island. But in fact he came to a land which already possessed a long Christian tradition. He found many of its people following the Christian faith which had been for generations the religion of their forefathers. There were at least seven bishops in the island, together with monasteries, abbots and men learned in the scriptures.[1] In Canterbury there was still standing a church, built during the Roman occupation of Britain (and therefore antedating Augustine by at least two hundred years and maybe more), dedicated, probably by Aethilberht's queen, Bertha, to St Martin.[2] It was here that St Augustine first said Mass and first preached to and baptized his English converts. Moreover he found dilapidated churches of the Roman period in many parts of Kent, for we are told that his conversion of the English King of Kent enabled him not only to build but to restore churches everywhere.[3]

Before he arrived Augustine knew nothing of what he would find. Indeed having left Rome on his journey, and having travelled only a short distance, he and his companions grew fearful of the dangers of their mission. Like the armies of the Emperor Claudius, who more than five hundred years earlier had mutinied when ordered to the

[1] Bede, *Hist. Ecc.* xi. 2. [2] Ibid. i. 26. [3] Ibid.

distant and virtually unknown land of Britain,[1] he and his companions took sudden fright. Just as the legions of Claudius had refused to march, appalled by their task of conquering and civilizing this unknown land, St Augustine and his followers were suddenly struck with terror at the thought of visiting the English nation, which they knew to be barbarous, fierce, pagan and warlike. St Augustine broke off his journey and hastened back to Rome, begging Pope Gregory to release him and his companions from so dangerous a mission. It was only after they had received a further exhortation from the Pope that the party, we must believe reluctantly, resumed their journey to this strange island, lying on the misty edge of the world.[2]

There was considerable irony in the events which followed. For it was not the barbarous and pagan nation of the English which received St Augustine with hostility. Indeed their king in Kent welcomed the missionaries in peace and friendship, allowing them to preach and to proselytize at will. On the contrary, it was the old Christian communities, in areas where the English had not yet penetrated, and where the old Romano-British culture still lingered, which resented the coming of this mission from Rome, and which disputed with bitterness St Augustine's authority.[3]

They saw his coming as an arrogant intrusion, and his avowed intention to convert the inhabitants of the island as an insult to their own constant faith. For they knew that Christian communities had dwelt in Britain for many centuries, and that by St Augustine's time the religion had been destroyed only in those regions that had suffered the full-scale invasion of the Angles, Saxons and Jutes from Germany. Certainly from the early fourth century, when under the Emperor Constantine Christianity had become the official religion of the Roman Empire, it had flourished in Britain as elsewhere. But it had taken root in the island even earlier. Legend and myth bear witness to a belief that it had come here in Apostolic times, within a few years of the Crucifixion. Archaeological and documentary evidence alike bear witness to the fact that Christianity was firmly established in Britain during the centuries before the coming of St Augustine.

The Christian Britons moreover were sure that Constantine the Great was himself half British and that his British mother, Helena, had been a devout Christian. Therefore to them the mission from

[1] Dio, lx. 19. [2] Bede, *Hist. Ecc.* i. 23. [3] Ibid. xi. 2.

Rome was totally unacceptable. It implied an ignorance in Rome of the ancient Christian traditions of Britain, and suggested that Rome was assuming a position of authority for which they could see no justification.

The purpose of this book is to trace the growth of Christianity in the island from the earliest times, through the hint of legend and speculation as well as through firmer evidence, to see how early it had been planted here and how it had flourished, long before Augustine set foot in Kent and established the see of Canterbury.

I

EARLY LINKS AND LEGENDS: THE FIRST AND SECOND CENTURIES

1

THE ROMAN CONQUEST

'GOD willed that all nations might be prepared to receive the doctrine of Christ, and accordingly His Providence subjected them to the emperor of Rome.' Thus wrote Origen (*c.* 185–*c.* 254), one of the most distinguished and most influential teachers of the early Church.

At the beginning of the Christian era Britain lay just outside the northern boundary of the Empire. North and west of a line drawn between the Tyne and the Exe, a 'highland zone' was inhabited by people of neolithic descent and Bronze Age culture. In the 'lowland zone', south and east of that line, a succession of Celtic invaders had introduced the later Iron Age civilization. During the first century B.C. one of these Celtic groups, known to history as the Belgae, had occupied the south-east—Hampshire, Berkshire and West Sussex. Their rule, or at least their hegemony, might have quickly extended over the entire lowland zone had not their advance been interrupted by the two invasions of Julius Caesar (55 and 54 B.C.). Caesar, however, was prevented by the unsettled state of Gaul, and later by the outbreak of civil war at home, from attempting the permanent occupation of Britain; and when King Cunobelin died (*c.* A.D. 41) the Belgic ascendancy was complete.

It was an open secret at Rome that Julius had intended ultimately to conquer Britain and annex it to the Empire. This explains the fact that at least until about 26 B.C. his heir Octavian (later known as Augustus) was repeatedly credited with the same intention by writers such as Horace and Virgil, who were expressing a widespread belief that the invasion of Britain was imminent.

Whether or not Augustus at any time entertained such a purpose, he seems to have decided that further expansion of the imperial boundaries had to be delayed in order that Rome's conquests in Gaul, Spain and the Illyrian provinces might be consolidated, and that was the policy he bequeathed to his successor Tiberius.

At no time, however, did Augustus publicly reject the plan to conquer Britain, which he must have known to be in the long run desirable and indeed inevitable. What he did was to make, or rather to countenance, excuses for its postponement; excuses which we have from the pen of Strabo.[1] Britain, according to the latter, was geographically so remote that it could be neither a danger nor an advantage to Rome: it lacked the strength necessary to invade Roman territory, and the duties on the busy trade between it and Gaul would yield considerably more than was likely to be derived from the island's tribute once the heavy cost of maintaining a garrison had been met. Moreover it was argued that several British rulers had made their peace with the Emperor and had thus rendered the island virtually a Roman province.

This is not the place to discuss the validity of those excuses, but the mention of trade is of great significance. Between the time of Julius and that of Augustus, traffic between Britain and Roman Gaul had led to a movement of 'Romanization' among the upper classes, at least in the southern parts of the island. Strabo himself enumerates the principal British exports as wheat, cattle, gold, silver, iron, hides, slaves and clever hunting dogs. To the imports he names (bracelets, necklaces, amber, glass and 'suchlike trifles') archaeological evidence has added several articles of luxury which illustrate the intensity of that Romanizing movement which was drawing Britain ever closer to the Continent: wine, Arretine pottery and rich Campanian metal-work. So extensive in fact was the commerce between Britain and Italy by way of Gaul that during the first three decades of the Christian era there grew up on the left bank of the Thames, on the site long since world famous as the city of London, a prosperous trading settlement.

By the year 40 it was clear to the imperial government that Britain would be able to pay her way as a province, and to this consideration there was added a new set of political circumstances. The long frontiers of the Empire were secure; the territories within them were peaceful; and troops were available for foreign service. Moreover dissension among the sons of Cunobelin had brought to light a strong anti-Roman party whose activity might easily have resulted in an armed attack on the Gallic coast and even a massacre of the numerous Roman traders resident in the island. Preparations for an invasion were made by the

[1] ii. 115–16; iv. 200.

Emperor Gaius (Caligula), but came to nothing; and it was not until the reign of his successor, Claudius, in A.D. 43, that the conquest was finally undertaken.

The military force entrusted with this task consisted of four legions and some auxiliary regiments of cavalry and infantry, numbering in all about forty thousand men, under the command of Aulus Plautius, who at that date was governor of Pannonia. The legions were as follows: II Augusta from Argentorate (Strasbourg), XIV Gèmina from Moguntiacum (Mainz), XX Valeria Victrix from its station near modern Cologne and IX Hispana from Pannonia.

These forces went aboard their transports at Gessoriacum (Boulogne) and landed in East Kent at what is now called Richborough, taking unawares the native levies under Caratacus and Togodumnus. Marching inland, they met with stiff resistance on the Medway, but a two-day battle—a most unusual occurrence in ancient warfare—ended in a Roman victory. At this point Claudius himself, a stammering pedant and the most unmilitary of emperors, arrived with reinforcements that included a detachment of the Praetorian Guards and an elephant corps! Under his nominal command, Camulodunum (Colchester), King Cunobelin's capital, was taken; Britain was now proclaimed a Roman province, with that town as its administrative centre and Plautius as its first governor. Several tribal chieftains made their submission, followed by others who had taken no part in the war. By the time of Plautius's recall in 47 most of the lowland zone had been occupied, and after another thirty years of intermittent fighting the highland zone also had been subjugated.

Britain, according to the view of Origen, was now ready to receive the doctrine of Christ, and it is natural to ask when, how and by whom Christianity was first introduced into the island. To these questions no certain answers can be returned; whether by the introduction of Christianity we mean the earliest presence here of individuals who happened also to be Christians, or, more correctly, the existence in the Roman province of more or less fully organized Christian communities. The most that can be said with any degree of confidence is that Britain was evangelized (possibly, but not probably, in the first century) [1] by

[1] It would seem unlikely that Britain was evangelized much before Gaul, about which our earliest information is that by the year 150 it possessed many Christian groups, one of which, Lyons, had been created a bishopric.

casual visits of Christians, mainly from Gaul. There are no good grounds for assuming an organized mission from the latter province or from elsewhere. St Irenaeus, for example, writing *circa* 176,[1] makes no mention of Britain in a list of Christian lands which includes the Celtic regions of northern Europe. The earliest concrete reference to Christianity in Britain is supplied by Tertullian [2] who, writing soon after the year 200, speaks of 'the places of the Britons not reached by the Romans but subject to Christ', and adds that 'Christ's name reigns there'. It is of course true that Tertullian, living in Africa, may have exaggerated both the extent and the social influence of the faith in the remote province of Britain, but his words are good evidence that Christianity existed in the island. As regards the much later stories of the Glastonbury mission of Joseph of Arimathaea and the subsequent request of King Lucius to Pope Eleutherius for missionaries, it is generally agreed that they lack firm historical foundation.

Nevertheless we are entitled to conjecture in the light of literary references and archaeological remains, provided that at every step we take account of historical fact, and also remember that a chain of reasoning is no stronger than its weakest link. If in the remainder of this Part our examination of those references and those remains yields largely negative results, it is hoped that their study will not be altogether fruitless or devoid of interest.

2

POMPONIA GRAECINA

IN A.D. 47, when Aulus Plautius returned to Rome after service as first governor of Britain, he was praised by Claudius and received the honour of an Ovation with triumphal ornaments, a curtailed form

[1] *Adv. haer.* i. 3.

[2] *Adv. Judaeos.* Gildas, the earliest surviving British historian (*c.* 517–70), admits his ignorance, since any documents that might have answered the question of Christian origins in Britain had been either destroyed by Saxon invaders or carried off by British emigrants.

of the old republican Triumph, which was now reserved to the Emperor alone. Ten years later, early in the reign of Nero, he found himself in what must have been an embarrassing situation. The affair is thus briefly narrated by Tacitus: 'Pomponia Graecina, a woman of illustrious birth and wife of Aulus Plautius who on his return from Britain entered the city with the pomp of an Ovation, was accused of having embraced a foreign superstition [*superstitionis externae rea*]. The matter was referred to her husband for judgment. Plautius, in conformity with ancient usage [*more maiorum*], called together a number of her relations, and in her presence sat in judgment on the conduct of his wife. He pronounced her innocent. She lived to a great age, forever unhappy. From the time when Julia, daughter of Drusus, was put to death through the wicked scheming of Messalina, she never laid aside her mourning, but lived in unremitting grief for a period of forty years, inconsolable for the loss of her friend. Throughout the reign of Claudius nothing could alleviate her sorrow, nor was her perseverance imputed to her as a crime; in the end it was the crown of her reputation.' [1]

This passage has led some to believe not only that Pomponia may have been a Christian, but also that she may have spent some time with her husband in Britain and made the first Christian converts there. This daring flight of fancy must be tested against such historical evidence as is available.

At the date in question, there were numerous Christians in Rome, most of them Jewish converts. Under Claudius they had not been clearly distinguished by the government except as a troublesome sect of Judaism. This is apparent from the fact that in A.D. 49 Claudius had expelled the Jews from Rome, following riots which Suetonius vaguely describes as having taken place *impulsante Chresto*, 'at the instigation of one Chrestos'—an apparent allusion to disturbances between Jews of the Synagogue and Jews of the Cross. It is likely, however, that by the time of Nero's accession in 54 the city authorities had recognized the Christians as an antisocial entity different from and independent of Jewry. It is also likely that among the populace of Rome there were already current some of those calumnies which had formerly been levelled against the Jews themselves and which, in their Christian context, are known to us from the pages of Justin, Athena-

[1] *Annals*, xiii. 32.

goras and other Apologists, and are brought together in a celebrated passage of Gibbon:

> It was asserted that a new-born infant, entirely covered over with flour, was presented, like some mystic symbol of initiation, to the knife of the proselyte, who unknowingly inflicted many a secret and mortal wound on the innocent victim of his error; that as soon as the cruel deed was perpetrated, the sectaries drank up the blood, greedily tore asunder the quivering members, and pledged themselves to eternal secrecy, by a mutual consciousness of guilt. It was as confidently affirmed that this inhuman sacrifice was succeeded by a suitable entertainment, in which intemperance served as a provocative to brutal lust; till, at the appointed moment, the lights were suddenly extinguished, shame was banished, nature was forgotten; and, as accident might direct, the darkness of the night was polluted by the incestuous commerce of sisters and brothers, of sons and of mothers.[1]

It was doubtless upon the strength of such rumours [2] that Tacitus and Suetonius, writing in the first quarter of the second century, spoke of the Christians in terms of unqualified abhorrence.

We may allow, therefore, that by A.D. 57 there was an organized Christian community in the Eternal City to which Pomponia could in theory have belonged, and that this community already enjoyed an unsavoury reputation. Tacitus does not expressly connect the charge of *superstitio externa* with Pomponia's long years of mourning for Julia. But he seems to do so indirectly, and indeed the morbid grief he describes might well have inclined its victim to seek solace or distraction in the rites (some of them orgiastic) of one or other of those many sects which proliferated throughout the Roman world and were considered immoral or potentially dangerous by the more conservative elements of society.

The central point in the argument of those who would make Christianity the object of Pomponia's choice is the word *superstitio*, used both by Tacitus [3] and by Suetonius [4] when describing the

[1] *Decline and Fall*, ch. xvi.

[2] They proceeded from misinterpretation of the eucharistic rite and the quasi-liturgical ceremony of the *agape*, which latter (or rather its abuse) had already begun to worry St Paul, *c.* A.D. 55 (I Cor. xi).

[3] *Ann.* xv. 44. [4] *Div. Nero* xvi.

Neronian persecution of A.D. 64. Both historians emphasize the foreign and detestable nature of the new religion, and both refer to the Christians by name. We should note, however, that their use of the word *superstitio* in this latter connection may derive from a common source, and that there is no reason to suppose that it could not have been applied in A.D. 57 to any sect whose beliefs and practices were alien to the traditions of Roman religion.

So far the evidence for Pomponia's Christian faith is unconvincing; but there is one remarkable feature of her trial that deserves consideration. At that time specific charges were normally required as the basis of action against adherents of a particular sect, not mere membership; yet Tacitus names the accusation in quite general terms—*superstitio externa*. His words, however, cannot be taken as proof that there *was* no specific charge. What could that charge have been? Was Pomponia perhaps accused under an old senatorial decree of consulting astrologers about the Emperor, or of refusal to take part in some official celebration? If so, we would expect the historian to make use of the facts as one more example of imperial tyranny. Highly significant for our purpose is the submission of her case to the jurisdiction of her husband. This, as Tacitus himself implies by the words *more maiorum*, was a return to a long obsolete judicial practice whereby family councils sat in judgment and passed sentence in cases of adultery. May not the gravamen of the charge against Pomponia have been adultery, a charge arising from her real or rumoured presence at what were believed to be the immoral rites of the Christian *agape* or love feast? We shall never know the truth. Study of the evidence leads to no more positive conclusion than that Pomponia Graecina certainly may have been a Christian, or may have had close relations with the Christian community in Rome.

As regards her assumed residence in Britain during her husband's government of the province, there is no evidence to support the view, which can indeed be shown to be altogether improbable. It is true that many wives of provincial governors did accompany their husbands. In the course of a debate in the Senate (A.D. 21), Caecina Severus, formerly legate of Moesia and then of Lower Germany, moved unsuccessfully that the practice should be disallowed.[1] But his remarks indicate that these women were for the most part viragoes, very different

[1] Tacitus, *Annals* iii. 33.

from the character of Pomponia as revealed by Tacitus. Secondly, though Britain was formally declared a province in A.D. 43, it was by no means settled at the time of Plautius's retirement four years later—circumstances in which the presence of his wife and her household appears in the last degree unlikely. Moreover the fact that Pomponia went into deep mourning on the execution of Julia in 43 suggests that she was not then with her husband in Pannonia,[1] a well-settled province. Is it probable that she would have chosen the wilds of Britain, whose prospect had daunted even the army before its embarkation in 43?

Before we leave the governorship of Aulus Plautius and the shadowy figure of his wife, two small points deserve notice. Neither is strictly relevant to our present study, but both would merit the attention of an historical novelist.

First, in the reign of Tiberius four legions constituted the garrison of Syria. One of them, XII Fulminata, was stationed at Raphaneae,[2] and remained there until the time of Nero. Now there is extant an inscription [3] from Antioch in Pisidia, dating from the reign of Claudius and commemorating a man named P. Anicius Maximus, who had served as quartermaster of Legion II Augusta in Britain and before that had been senior centurion of the Twelfth. Hence in the earliest days of the Roman occupation there was present in Britain a high-ranking officer who could have (no more than that) met and talked with men who had played a part in the Crucifixion.

Next, a Roman woman, unlike her menfolk, bore only two names: first that of the *gens* to which her father or her mother belonged, and secondly the *cognomen* of the person on whom in law she depended (usually husband or father). Now the father of Agricola, who was governor of Britain from 78 until 85, was named Julius Graecinus.[4]

He appears to have written a book on vines [5] and to have been the

[1] We must assume, for there is no documentary proof, that she was indeed his wife during the years of his command in Britain.

[2] Josephus, *B.J.* vii. 1. 3.

[3] Dessau, *Inscriptiones Latinae Selectae*, 269.

[4] Quoted by Columella. He was put to death by Gaius (A.D. 39 or 40). His wife was Julia Procilla.

[5] His agricultural interests were no doubt inherited by his son, hence the *cognomen* Agricola.

son of another Graecinus, who is twice addressed by Ovid.[1] According to Tacitus, Pomponia Graecina lived forty years in mourning from A.D. 43, and died at a great age. Assuming her to have been about thirty at the time of her husband's appointment to Britain, she was born *circa* A.D. 13. No chronological difficulty is involved in seeing her as a daughter of Ovid's Graecinus, since the *Amores* appeared soon after 16 B.C., and books 1–3 of *Pontic Letters* were written between A.D. 12 and 13. Upon this assumption, therefore, Pomponia was aunt of Agricola and related to the historian Tacitus, who married Agricola's daughter in A.D. 77.

3

THE CIRENCESTER WORD SQUARE

AMONG the archaeological evidence for the presence of Christianity in Roman Britain, there is one item that may date from the first century.

Modern Cirencester stands on the site of the Roman city of *Corinium*. This was a large and prosperous town, not founded by the Romans, but developed by them from a tribal capital already in existence before they came. It lay on an important crossroads. From *Calleva Atrebatum* (Silchester), another important tribal capital (near Reading), a Roman road ran through *Corinium* to *Glevum* (Gloucester). From *Isca*, the modern Exeter, another tribal capital, a second great road, the Fosse Way, passed through *Corinium* on its long alignment across the midlands through *Ratae* (Leicester) to *Lindum* (Lincoln) and the north.

In 1868 there was found at Cirencester a small piece of wall plaster from a Roman building. The wall had been painted a dull red, and scratched upon it in neat capital letters was the following word square:

---

[1] *Am.* 2. 10; *Pont.* 1. 6.

R O T A S
O P E R A
T E N E T
A R E P O
S A T O R

This can be read line by line horizontally from the top; or vertically from the top left-hand corner; or horizontally from the bottom right-hand corner taking each line right to left; or vertically from the same point, taking each line from bottom to top. In all cases, the same sentence is read:

ROTAS OPERA TENET AREPO SATOR

The meaning of these words is not clear. However, the generally accepted translation is:

'The sower Arepo holds the wheels carefully.'

An alternative translation has been suggested:

'The sower guides the wheels for the plough carefully.'

This is based on the assumption that AREPO is formed from a Celtic word for a wheeled plough. In any case, no precise meaning can be given to the sentence itself, and the significance of the word square must be sought outside the literal value of the words. It was in 1926 that Felix Grosser [1] suggested an explanation that is now generally accepted. He showed that all the letters of the square can be used to write the words 'Pater Noster' twice, provided that this is done in the form of a cross, with the single letter N at the intersection. This leaves unused two A's and two O's. These are the Latin equivalents of the Greek letters Alpha and Omega that were used as a symbol of Christ, echoing the words in the Revelation of St John: 'I am Alpha and Omega, the beginning and the ending, saith the Lord, which is, and which was, and which is to come, the Almighty.' Thus the solution of the word square is:

---

[1] *Archiv für Religionswissenschaft*. xxix. 1926.

A
·
P
A
T
E
R
A · P A T E R N O S T E R · O
O
S
T
E
R
·
O

The word square can now be seen as a cryptic reference to Christianity, dating from a period before that religion could be safely professed.

Just before Grosser's solution a further version of the square was discovered in 1925 [1] in one of the houses at Pompeii. Yet another was discovered in the same city in 1936.[2] We know that Pompeii was destroyed during the eruption of Vesuvius in A.D. 79, so that the versions of the word square found there must date to that year or earlier. They might indeed date to the sixties, when Nero was persecuting the Christians and when it would have been logical for secret and cryptic references to Christianity to be devised. That the use of this word square was widespread is shown by the discovery of four versions at Dura-Europos on the Euphrates, which was in Roman hands from A.D. 165 to *circa* 257.[3]

The British square may of course be of the second or third centuries; but if it dates, like its counterparts from Pompeii, to the latter part of

[1] *N.D.S.* 1929, 449. No. 112.
[2] Rand: *Accad. Pont. Arch. Rom.* xii. 1936.
[3] J. M. C. Toynbee, *Journal of Brit. Arch. Ass.* xvi. 1953.

the first century, we may here have evidence of Christians in *Corinium* during that period.

4

GLASTONBURY

THE great abbey of St Mary at Glastonbury, in Somerset, appears to have developed from a small wattle church built by an unknown founder some time before the year 633, when it was covered with boarding and a lead roof by Paulinus. It was not until about five centuries later that a wealth of legend, belonging rather to the realm of fiction than of genuine tradition, began to gather round Glastonbury, centring upon Joseph of Arimathaea and linking the spot with the Passion and Resurrection of Christ.

Joseph, who looms large in the closing pages of the gospels, was a native of Ramathain, and all four evangelists are agreed that he buried Jesus. According to St Mark [1] he was an 'honourable counsellor' awaiting the kingdom of God. At the hour of Christ's death the Sabbath was approaching, and had not Joseph intervened the body would have been left on the cross for more than twenty-four hours, in violation of Deuteronomy xxi. 3, which ordered that the body of a criminal hung upon a tree should not remain there overnight. Joseph went to Pilate and obtained permission to bury the body, which he did with all the care that time allowed. In the light of St Mark's report there is no reason to suppose that he was a disciple of Jesus; respect for the Mosaic law would have been sufficient motive, though his approach to Pilate becomes more intelligible if we see him as a member of the Sanhedrin or as acting on their instructions. Nor does St Mark lead us to suppose that choice of the tomb was dictated by any consideration other than its handiness—to look for one farther afield might have entailed breach of the Sabbath.

[1] Mark xv. 42–6.

St Matthew, however,[1] tells us that Joseph was a wealthy man and a disciple of Jesus, and that the tomb was one that he had recently had made for himself. St Luke [2] states that he was in fact a member of the Sanhedrin, who had not consented to the condemnation, and describes the sepulchre as rock-hewn and one in which 'never before man was laid'. Finally, St John [3] says that he was a secret disciple; that Nicodemus helped him with the burial; and that the sepulchre was situated in a garden. In the second-century apocryphal *Gospel of Peter* Joseph is a friend of Pilate and arranges with him for the burial before the Crucifixion. In the no less apocryphal *Gospel of Nicodemus* (perhaps of the fourth century), known also as the *Acts of Pilate*, he is imprisoned by the Jews after the burial and set free by the risen Christ.

About nine hundred years later a mid thirteenth-century interpolation in William of Malmesbury's *De antiquitate Glastonensis ecclesiae* tells us that Joseph of Arimathaea came to Glastonbury at the head of twelve missionaries sent by the Apostle Philip. Malmesbury's original work, written *circa* 1129–30, makes no mention of Joseph, and represents the wattle church as having been built by missionaries from Rome.[4] The author was aware of an earlier story, but would not commit himself to it.

However, he does tell us another story. He writes that St David was in Glastonbury in the late fifth or early sixth century, and planned to rededicate the church. But Jesus came to him in a dream and forbade him to do so, saying that the 'Church had already been dedicated by Himself in honour of His Mother, and that the ceremony was not to be profaned by human repetition'. William of Malmesbury, like other medieval historians, lacked reliable sources and the training to discriminate between them, and this story of St David remains without corroboration, but it serves to show that in the Middle Ages there was widespread belief in the Apostolic origins of the British Church.

If St David cannot be proved to have visited Glastonbury, he was at least contemporary with it, since he lived at around the time when,

[1] Matt. xxvii. 57–60. [2] Luke xxiii. 50–4. [3] John xix. 38–43.

[4] By those missionaries, who, as we shall see, were alleged to have been sent by the Pope at the request of King Lucius. Malmesbury's interpolator makes them not builders, but restorers of the original church.

according to another source, there was a Christian community there. An old Welsh poem, the *Triedd Ynis Pritein*, speaks of three places in Britain where choirs sing day and night continually; Glastonbury is one, and Amesbury is another. As Amesbury was destroyed in the middle of the sixth century, the poem must have been written before then.

Among the details of the Glastonbury legend, which was rapidly embellished, was Joseph's planting of his staff (or a cutting from the Crown of Thorns) on Wearyall Hill near by, which took root and flourished ever afterwards.

Celebrated above all other stories concerning Joseph is the one that speaks of his having brought to Britain the most glorious and most mystical of all relics—the Holy Grail, the wine-cup used at the Last Supper. The Glastonbury sources do not link Joseph with the Grail; the earliest extant work to do so is Robert de Boron's *Joseph d'Arimathie*, written probably *circa* 1200 or a little later. According to this poem Joseph of Arimathaea is entrusted with the sacred vessel, which is destined to be taken by his brother-in-law, Bron, to the *vaus d'Avaron*, the vale of Avalon, which is identified by Giraldus Cambrensis and Roger de Coggeshall with Glastonbury.

That is all the evidence we have for the story of Joseph's coming to Britain, and from an historian's point of view it must be reckoned as of little value. But why did such a man come to be associated during the Middle Ages with Roman Britain and with Glastonbury of all unlikely places? The answer is probably to be sought in that love of poetic invention displayed by so many medieval hagiographers. A cynic might add that in an age when the techniques of historical criticism had yet to be discovered, and when the majority of men wallowed in a sea of credulity (later called 'simple piety'), the clergy were not averse from linking their Churches, as a matter of good business no less than of devotion, with one or other of the great New Testament figures. Witness Denys the Areopagite in Paris! By the end of the twelfth century Glastonbury had long since become one of the oldest and most renowned religious centres in western Europe. What more natural, therefore, than to trace the origins of so ancient and so famous a shrine back to the first owner of the Holy Sepulchre—the goal of the Crusades—to the man in whose arms had lain the body of the World's Redeemer? No other Church had appropriated him;

and there for all to see grew the mysterious Thorn that flowered in midwinter as well as in the spring. Whence could that tree have sprung if not from the terrible diadem used for the coronation in the guard-room of Antonia; and who could have brought the Crown if not he who must have taken it from the God-Man's head?

5

KING LUCIUS

IN THE sixties of the first century, that is to say a mere twenty years after the conquest of Britain by Claudius, Roman rule was almost swept from the island by the bloody and merciless campaign of Boudicca, Queen of the Iceni. Roman citizens, and those Britons who had acquiesced in the occupation, were put to the sword, crucified or sent to the stake by the vengeful army of the Iceni. It is said that seventy thousand perished.[1] When fresh troops landed from the Continent, the Roman governor, Suetonius Paulinus, began a terrible campaign of reprisals. Only with the arrival of Petronius Turpilanus, a more humane governor, was Roman order finally restored.

Thereafter the peaceful Romanization of the island was resumed, and the second century was a time of orderly progress and development. It was a century of great emperors—Trajan, Hadrian, Antoninus Pius and Marcus Aurelius the philosopher. It was also a period when Britain's intimate contacts with Rome increased. The figure of Britannia appeared on Roman coins. The Emperor Hadrian travelled extensively in the island,[2] and the last emperor of the century, Septimius Severus, died at York.[3] Trade between Britain and the Continent increased, and people and ideas moved freely across the Channel.

[1] Tacitus, *Annals*, xiv. 34.
[2] *Hist. Aug.* 'Adrianus Imp.'; C.I.L. iii. 4279.
[3] Ibid. 'Severus Imp.'.

So far as Christianity in the province is concerned, we find ourselves once more in a world of make-believe. But whereas the tale of Glastonbury is suffused with poetry and cannot be formally disproved, that of King Lucius has no such charm and runs counter to the facts of history.

'In the year of our Lord's incarnation 156', writes Bede, 'Marcus Antoninus Verus [Marcus Aurelius] . . . was made Emperor, together with his brother Aelius Commodus [his adoptive brother L. Aelius Verus]. In their time, whilst Eleutherus [or Eleutherius], a holy man, presided over the Roman Church, Lucius, King of the Britons, sent a letter to him, entreating that by his command he might be made a Christian. He soon obtained his pious request, and the Britons preserved the faith which they had received, uncorrupted and entire, in peace and tranquillity until the time of the Emperor Diocletian.'[1]

Nennius, writing *circa* 796 and using sources other than Bede, tells us that 'after one hundred and sixty-seven years from the coming of Christ, the British king, Lucius, with all the minor kings of the entire British people, received baptism, a mission having been sent by the Roman emperors and by the Roman Pope Eucharisto'.[2]

Now Bede states that among his own sources were extracts from the archives of the Holy See, brought back from Rome by a London priest named Nothelm and handed to him on the advice of Abbot Albinus of Canterbury. Sure enough, in the *Liber Pontificalis*[3] there is mention of a letter from *Lucio Britannio rege*, written to Pope Eleutherius and asking for missionaries to convert his people.

Apart from inconsistencies between those three documents, so far so good. But let us now take a look at each in turn: (1) Bede places the accession of Marcus Aurelius and Lucius Verus in 156. The correct

[1] *Hist. Ecc.* I. 4.

[2] *Hist. Brit.* xxii. Nennius identifies Lucius with Lleur Mawr, a chieftain in South Wales; the two names agree in expressing the idea of brightness. The Welsh triads and genealogies, of uncertain date, make Lleur founder of the Church of Llandaff, and give the names Dyfan, Ffagan, Medwy and Elfan (possible all real persons) as those of the missionaries sent by Eleutherus. The Book of Llandaff names Dyfan and Ffagan as Lucius's own messengers to Rome. The Welsh stories provide little detail, and there would be nothing *inherently* improbable in their account if earlier authority for Lucius's existence were available, which, as we shall see, it is not.

[3] Ed. L. Duchesne, vol. 1, 1884.

date is 161. Moreover, although the regnal years of the popes before Calixtus I (217/18–222) are conjectural, the traditional dates of Eleutherius are 175–89—a rather long cry from 156 and even from 161. (2) It is quite inconceivable that either Marcus, or Verus, or both, should have been parties to a missionary undertaking. Again, there never was a Pope Eucharisto; the nearest approach to such a name in the list of Roman pontiffs is Evaristo, but his traditional dates are 97–105 (or 101–5). (3) Here now is the final undoing of the story. The section of the *Liber Pontificalis* in which King Lucius appears was not written until about the middle of the sixth century, and there is no earlier record whatsoever of that king's existence.

By far the most likely explanation of the tale is to be found in the opinion of modern scholars, who are generally agreed that the word *Britannio* in the text of the *Liber Pontificalis* was written in error by some medieval scribe for Britio, which was in fact one of the strongholds of Lucius Aelius Septimius Abgar, an early Christian king of Edessa in the north-west of Mesopotamia, who laboured for the conversion of his people in the mid second century. The first two of his Roman names were doubtless assumed as a compliment to the Emperor L. Aelius Verus, whose forces, under C. Avidius Cassius, overran Abgar's realm of Osroëne (163–5), which then became a Roman dependency.

2

CHURCH AND STATE TO THE THIRD CENTURY

1

NERO TO SEPTIMIUS SEVERUS

BEFORE taking our first look at Christian Britain in the full light of history, we must pause here to explain briefly the situation of the Church under the imperial government.

From the reign of Nero onwards Christianity was a proscribed religion; but it must not be supposed that the authorities were at all times and everywhere active against its adherents. Seldom indeed, before the reign of Decius, was a general persecution initiated by the Emperor. The prosperity of the Church depended usually upon the whims of a governor or, more often, upon the passions of a city mob; for we have to remember that Christianity was for long essentially an urban religion with little influence in the countryside. The sudden upsurges of feeling against the Christians were probably due in most cases to groups of local agitators whose followers would have been unable to tell an inquirer precisely against what or on behalf of what they were demonstrating—a phenomenon not unfamiliar today. Sometimes such riots might spread like wildfire through a whole province; the governor was responsible to the Emperor for the maintenance of order, and he had in such circumstances to take stern measures against a community that was in any case technically illegal.

After the brief persecution under Nero, which arose from the Emperor's determination to find a scapegoat for the Great Fire of Rome, and which appears to have been confined to the capital, the Christian communities seem to have lived more or less undisturbed until Domitian struck at all whom he suspected of hostility to himself—the aristocracy, the philosophers, the astrologers and finally the Jews and Christians. By this time Christianity had begun to climb the social scale; M. Acilius Glabrio (consul in 91) may have been a Christian, and it is almost certain that the Emperor's cousin Flavius Clemens and the latter's wife Domitilla both suffered for their faith.

By this time also the Church had begun to increase not only in numbers, and in the quality of its membership, but also in power and pretensions. Its close-knit hierarchical organization might be viewed as an attempt to create a 'state within the State'; while its absolute and unshakable refusal to take part in the official worship soon came to be considered as evidence of disloyalty.

In the year 112 the younger Pliny was governor of Pontus and Bithynia. He had never taken part in judicial proceedings against the Christians. Accordingly he was completely ignorant as to the nature of their guilt, as to the kind of evidence upon which they should be convicted and as to the penalties that such convictions entailed. He therefore submitted to the Emperor Trajan an impartial and, to some extent, a favourable account of the Christians, and asked for guidance.[1] Now the fact that Pliny was a distinguished barrister, a member of the Senate, an ex-consul and a friend of eminent people in every walk of life suggests that at the time of his appointment to Bithynia there were no general laws or decrees of the Senate in force against the Christians; that neither Trajan nor his predecessors had publicly declared their intentions concerning the new sect; and that whatever legal steps had already been taken against the Christians, there was none of sufficient authority to establish any illuminating precedent for the conduct of a Roman magistrate.

The answer of Trajan,[2] says Gibbon, 'instead of displaying the implacable zeal of an Inquisitor, anxious to discover the most minute particles of heresy and exulting in the number of his victims', acknowledged the difficulty of establishing any general plan. The Emperor, however, laid down two rules: (1) Christians are not to be sought out, but once legally convicted they must be punished; (2) the magistrate must take no account of information laid by anonymous accusers.

This policy was followed by Hadrian, whose edict has been preserved by Eusebius:[3] 'If anyone accuse the Christians and prove that they have done anything contrary to the law, judge them according to the crime they have committed; if they have been calumniated, punish the calumniator.' That the antichristian laws continued to be applied under Hadrian's two successors, Antoninus Pius and Marcus Aurelius, is clear from the execution of Justin Martyr in A.D. 161 and a

[1] Pliny, *Epist.* x. 97. [2] Ibid. 98. [3] *Hist. Eccl.* iv. 9.

severe persecution of the faithful at Lyons and Vienne in A.D. 177.[1]

Strangely enough, under the monster Commodus, Marcus's son and successor, the Church, according to Eusebius,[2] enjoyed profound tranquillity. This appears to have been due largely to the Emperor's concubine Marcia, who, if not herself a believer, was certainly a friend and helper of the Christians, even to the extent of securing the release of many who had been condemned to the mines in Sardinia.

The tyranny of Commodus, however, was such that in A.D. 192 he was assassinated. Marcia took a leading part in the conspiracy; and if Eusebius speaks the truth concerning her faith, she may qualify as the first Christian murderess on record!

Between 193 and 211 (when he died at York) the throne was occupied by L. Septimius Severus, an African. His wife Julia Domna, his sister-in-law Julia Maesa and her daughter Julia Mammaea were all intensely curious in matters of religions. It is not surprising therefore that during most of his reign Christianity flourished undisturbed and was even represented in the imperial household. Tertullian states that Caracalla, son of Severus, was 'brought up on Christian milk',[3] a reference to the fact that the boy's nurse and, later, his tutor were both Christians. Moreover it is said that the Emperor himself believed that when gravely ill he had derived some benefit from the holy oil with which one of his servants had anointed him. Furthermore, mob violence was firmly checked; and the magistrates contented themselves with an annual present from the churches as the price or reward of their

[1] There is a solitary but celebrated reference to Christianity in Marcus's *Meditations* (xi. 3): 'How admirable is the soul which is ready and resolved, if it must this moment be released from the body, to be either extinguished or scattered or to persist. This resolve too must arise from a specific decision, not out of unreasoned resistance like the Christians but after reflexion and with dignity, and so as to convince others, without histrionic display.'

The passage is almost always misinterpreted. Marcus refers to the enthusiasm for martyrdom, which was characteristic of many Stoics as well as Christians, and he takes the latter simply as an example of those who choose death on grounds of private judgment. He is not condemning the Christians, as is commonly alleged by those who have never read the Greek text; he is illustrating a point by means of an example which has a peculiar poignancy for the Christian reader.

[2] *Hist. Eccl.* v. 21. [3] *Ad Scap.* iv.

moderation. But in A.D. 202, while he was in Palestine, Severus issued an edict banning any religious propaganda by Jews or Christians. This new law was not directed at existing Christian communities, who, it was clear, were left free to continue their worship in peace. Priests could teach their flocks, visit the faithful in prison and help them in the courts. Their assemblies and elections were left undisturbed.[1] It was only the preaching of the faith to non-Christians that was forbidden.

The edict was interpreted variously by the governors of the several provinces. The first execution took place in Carthage,[2] and the persecution quickly spread throughout the Empire.

The wide geographical extent of the official campaign against proselytizing is a measure of the manner in which Christianity had spread in one hundred and sixty years from the Crucifixion.

The public actions of Severus against the Christians seem to be in conflict with his general goodwill towards the Church, and at least one early Christian writer found this contradiction bewildering and went out of his way to find an explanation. Tertullian [3] tells us that Severus acted under great provocation. On one of his military expeditions the Emperor noticed a soldier who was carrying in his hand a crown of honour that he had won. Those crowns were the equivalent of modern medals, and by carrying it and not wearing it the soldier was acting contrary to normal custom and discipline. Asked why he was not wearing his decoration the soldier answered that he was a Christian. Not only was Severus a strict disciplinarian, but he attached the greatest importance to the maintenance of loyalty and good order in the army. This incident therefore enraged him, and Tertullian reports that it was this that prompted his measures against the Christians. But the prevailing sympathy towards the religion could not be immediately changed, and many magistrates tempered the law with mercy. Some refused to put to death those whom they considered innocent of any crime, and dismissed the charges brought in their courts.[4]

That Tertullian sought thus to explain away the persecution under Septimius Severus, and did not recognize the persecution as invalidating the Emperor's good name, shows how high that reputation stood among the Christians.

[1] Eusebius, *Hist. Eccl.* vi. 3
[2] Ibid. vi. 2.
[3] *De Cor. Mil.*
[4] Tertullian, *Ad Scap.* 5.

2
ALEXANDER SEVERUS TO DECIUS

WITHIN eleven years of the death of Septimius Severus three emperors had ascended the imperial throne and perished by the sword: Caracalla, Macrinus, Elagabalus, none of whom was noticeably antichristian. It can therefore be said that, except during the reign of Maximin (235–8), the Church enjoyed a calm of thirty-nine years. During that period two sovereigns are of particular interest to the historian of Christianity: Alexander Severus (222–35) and Philip 'the Arabian' (244–9).

Alexander, successor of Elagabalus and son of Julia Mammaea, was the first Roman emperor to give the Christians open support.[1] Of Eastern origin, careless of old Roman traditions and completely dominated by the well-meant but stifling mother-love of Julia Mammaea, who was deeply interested in, though never an adherent of, the Christian faith, Alexander dreamed of a syncretistic religion. He is said to have placed in his private chapel an image of Christ together with those of Apollonius of Tyana,[2] Abraham, Orpheus and the least disreputable of the Caesars.

It is difficult, however, to believe with the *Historia Augusta* that he once decided to build a temple dedicated to Christ, so that Christians might worship openly and follow their cult publicly as did the devotees of all other religions in Rome,[3] but was dissuaded from doing so by some of his advisers, who argued that if the Christians were given such official encouragement their religion would soon become widespread, and all other temples would be deserted. Nevertheless Alexander's

[1] Our knowledge of Alexander Severus is dependent chiefly on the life in the *Historia Augusta*, a compilation dating from the late fourth century and intended as propaganda for Julian 'the Apostate'. Much of the *Historia* is gravely suspect unless corroborated by other evidence.

[2] It was at the request of Alexander's great-aunt, the Empress Julia Domna, that Philostratus wrote the *Life of Apollonius of Tyana*.

[3] *Hist. Aug.*

relations with the Christians were frequent and more than benevolent. Julius Africanus visited Rome at the Emperor's request and helped to build up a library. Origen was a friend of Julia Mammaea,[1] to whom St Hippolytus addressed a treatise on the Resurrection. Moreover it is said that, wishing to subject the choice of magistrates to popular approval, Alexander cited as an example the procedure adopted by the Christians in the case of candidate for ordination. Finally, in a lawsuit concerning some property between the Church of Rome and the Corporation of Innkeepers, Alexander gave judgment for the former.[2]

It is certain that during the reign of Philip 'the Arabian' (244–9) no official measures were enforced against the Church. Origen addressed several letters to Philip as well as to his wife and mother. A letter written by Denys of Alexandria, preserved by Eusebius,[3] and mentioning those princes who were commonly supposed to be Christians, clearly alludes to Philip and his family; it affords contemporary evidence that such a belief was prevalent, though Denys himself speaks with some diffidence concerning the truth of that belief. At all events, the unconcealed favour of the Emperor towards the Christians, and his constant respect for the ministers of the Church, gave colour to the contemporary rumour that he had been converted to the faith, and afforded some grounds for the subsequent fable[4] that he had, by order of St Babylas, Bishop of Antioch, done penance for the murder of Gordian, which had brought him to the throne. We cannot go so far as to believe that Philip was officially a Christian, but a secret adherence to the religion is not altogether impossible. His birthplace, Hauran in Trachonitis, on the borders of Palestine, was largely Christian; the man himself appears to have been at most times

[1] According to Eusebius (vi. 21), and St Jerome (*Script. Eccles.* 54), on one occasion when the Empress Mammaea was passing through Antioch, she expressed a desire to converse with the celebrated Origen, the fame of whose piety and learning had spread throughout the eastern provinces. Origen obeyed the flattering invitation and, says Gibbon, 'though he could not expect to succeed in the conversion of an artful and ambitious woman, she listened with pleasure to his eloquent exhortations, and honourably dismissed him to his retirement in Palestine'. (Ch. xvi.)

[2] Very few popular outbursts of antichristian violence are recorded in the reign of Alexander. The worst occurred in Rome on 14th October 222, and resulted in the murder of Pope Calixtus I.

[3] *Hist. Eccl.* vii. 10. [4] *Hist. Eccl.* vi. 34.

charitable and gentle; the crime to which he owed his pre-eminence may be considered as one of those deplorable features of an age not unlike our own; and something more than mere benevolence may have lain behind the gesture of allowing Pope Fabian to bring back the relics of his predecessor Pontian, who had been exiled to Sardinia by Maximin.

If the Christian subjects of Philip imagined that abiding peace had at last dawned, they were quickly undeceived. The death of their benefactor was followed by a new system of government so oppressive to the Church that in no long time her tribulation since the reign of Domitian came to be regarded as an age of bliss, compared with the savage treatment they received during the brief reign of Decius (249–51).[1] The character of Decius is incompatible with a theory that he was inspired by nothing loftier than petty resentment against the beneficiaries of his predecessor, and it is more reasonable to suppose that his determination to rid the Empire of what he viewed as an upstart crowd of knaves was part of a larger scheme whose purpose was to restore the manners and religion of ancient Rome. The bishops of the most important sees were torn from their flocks by exile or by death. The throne of Peter itself remained vacant from the martyrdom of Pope Fabian (20th January 250) until the election of Cornelius (4th June 251); and we learn from Eusebius [2] that, in the opinion of the Christians, the Emperor would have been more ready to tolerate a competitor for the purple than a bishop in the capital.

At the instigation of the praetorian prefect Macrianus, who was addicted to Egyptian superstitions, the persecution of Decius was revived under Valerian (253–60) during the last three and a half years of his reign. His most famous victim was St Cyprian. But his son Gallienus (260–3) restored peace to the Church. The Christians were granted free exercise of their religion by an edict addressed to the bishops in terms that seemed to recognize their office and status; the old antichristian laws, though still in force, were allowed to fall into disuse and the disciples of Christ began to enjoy more than forty years of unbroken prosperity.

[1] Lactantius, *De Mortibus, Persecutorum* 3, 4.
[2] *Hist. Eccl.* vi. 34.

3

THE FOURTH CENTURY

1
THE FIRST BRITISH MARTYRS

IN A.D. 285, a year after his accession, the Emperor Diocletian took a colleague in the person of his fellow soldier Maximian, at first with the junior title of Caesar. Less than twelve months later he promoted him to the rank of Augustus, co-equal with his own. Maximian was to govern Italy and the west, while Diocletian administered the eastern portion of the Empire. Not long afterwards an officer named Carausius, commander of a Roman fleet stationed at Gessoriacum (Boulogne), managed to usurp the imperial authority in Britain and on the opposite coast of Gaul, and in 289 the two Augusti saw fit for the time being to recognize him as their associate.

In 293 the government of the Empire was subdivided by the appointment of two junior emperors known as Caesars—Galerius subordinate to Diocletian, Constantius to Maximian. The arrangement was that, when an Augustus died or abdicated, his Caesar would take his rank and choose someone else to follow him in the junior station. The area of Constantius's jurisdiction included Britain, Gaul and Spain. That same year Carausius was murdered by Allectus, his minister of finance, at a moment when Constantius had begun to lay plans for the invasion and recovery of Britain. This was accomplished in 296. The praetorian prefect Asclepiodotus defeated and killed Allectus somewhere in Hampshire, while the Caesar himself landed at Richborough, marched on London and overwhelmed the remnant of the usurper's motley array. A medal shows the conqueror arriving at one of the city gates greeted by a kneeling figure and encircled with the legend *Redditor Lucis Aeternae*.

In 297, in accordance with Diocletian's new territorial system, Britain became one of the twelve dioceses which now constituted the Roman Empire, and was itself divided into four provinces named Britannia Prima, Britannia Secunda, Maxima Caesariensis (after Galerius Maximianus) and Flavia Caesariensis (after Flavius

Constantius). The diocese was governed by a *vicarius* directly responsible to the praetorian prefect of Gaul, and each of the four provinces by a subordinate official.

Meanwhile Constantius set about the task of reorganization. He repaired Hadrian's Wall, rebuilt the fortress of York, repaired the walls and public buildings of several towns and, above all, took steps to meet the threat of Frankish and Saxon piracy by fortifying the south-eastern coast from the Wash to the Isle of Wight—a line famous in history as the Saxon Shore.

Six years passed during which, though Galerius was known to entertain antichristian sentiments, Diocletian showed himself almost entirely favourable to the Church. Then there began the last and most terrible of all the persecutions, inaugurated by a series of four edicts (the first dated 24th February 303) each more comprehensive and more savage than the last.

Into the complicated motives and lurid details of that persecution, which continued more or less uninterruptedly in some parts of the Empire for eight years, we need not enter here, since our concern is not with the Empire but with Britain alone. The whole story may be read in the eighth book of Eusebius's *Ecclesiastical History*, and the eleventh to the fifteenth chapters of Lactantius, *De Mortibus Persecutorum*.

How long the decrees took to reach Britain from Nicomedia is doubtful. In spite of a highly efficient postal service, fifty days elapsed before the first was published in Syria, and nearly four months before it was announced to the cities of Africa. Gibbon reasonably suggests that 'the delay may perhaps be imputed to the cautious temper of Diocletian, who had yielded a reluctant consent to the measures of persecution, and who was desirous of trying the experiment under his more immediate eye before he gave way to the disorders and discontent which it must inevitably occasion in the distant provinces'.[1]

Constantius appears to have acted with all the leniency compatible with his own safety and his obedience to the senior emperors, the Augusti; and when he succeeded Maximian in 305 he declined to continue in a course so repugnant to his nature. We learn, however,

[1] The attitude of Constantius is reflected in a meeting of nineteen bishops and twenty-four presbyters from all parts of Spain in the Synod of Elvira (*c.* 305).

from Gildas,[1] writing in the sixth century, that in Britain many churches were destroyed, but that these were later rebuilt and many new ones erected. The absence of archaeological evidence to confirm his statement is of no significance. As we shall see later, the Christian communities were poor, and their churches were therefore probably constructed of the flimsiest materials.

The most glorious episode in the history of the British Church during that terrible ordeal is the story of Britain's protomartyr. The city of Verulamium, lying some nineteen miles north-west of London on the great highway of Watling Street, which linked—and still links—the south-east coast with the remote mountains of northern Wales, had for long been one of the proudest centres of the Roman province. As early as the late first century, when Agricola was governor, important public buildings had been erected there. Among the Christians in the city at the time of Diocletian's persecution was a man named Albanus, now known as St Alban.[2] The magistrates, here as elsewhere, were carrying out orders by arresting all Christian bishops and priests. One such priest, an unhappy fugitive from the authorities, came to Alban's house and sought refuge there from his pursuers. Alban gave the priest shelter and, to help him on his way, exchanged clothes with him. So it was Alban, now dressed as a Christian priest, who was arrested. He staunchly refused to betray the fugitive and was himself condemned to death. According to tradition, he was taken for execution to a small hill outside the city; the route lay across a stream which, by divine intervention, parted as the Red Sea had parted in former days, so that Alban walked dry-foot to his martyrdom. He was executed on the hill, and tradition says that the altar in St Albans Cathedral was built on the very spot where he met his death.[3] He is the protomartyr of Britain, the first British Christian whose name is recorded as having suffered death for the faith.[4] Later, when the Roman city had decayed, and when the English had built their new town a little apart from the desolate acres of Roman ruins, they named it after Alban, who was already revered as a martyr before the middle of the

[1] *De excidio Britanniae*, x, xi.

[2] The later tradition that he had served in the Roman Army dates from a time when Britons supposed all Romans in the island to have been soldiers.

[3] Here in 793 King Offa founded the famous monastery.

[4] Bede, *Eccl. Hist.* i. 4.

fifth century. The name of the city of St Albans is his lasting memorial.

He was one of many; Bede gives us the names of two other men who suffered martyrdom in Britain—Aaron and Julius, both of Caerleon.

2

CONSTANTINE: THE BEGINNINGS

THE Emperor Diocletian was not a man who conferred office upon any man without taking security for the recipient's good behaviour. So when Galerius and Constantius were created Caesars in 293, the former married Diocletian's daughter Valeria, while the latter was obliged to put away his wife Helena and marry Theodora, daughter of Maximian, and also to place Constantine, his son by Helena, as a virtual hostage at the court of Nicomedia. There the young man learned much of the art of warfare and, no doubt, something of the wiles of government.

Helena was for long a favourite in Britain and later in England, where many churches are dedicated in her name; and it is therefore worth while to record here the few facts which are known, or which can be surmised, about her life. She was born *circa* 247, probably at Drepanum, a town on the Gulf of Nicomedia which Constantine later renamed Helenopolis. She is commonly supposed to have been the concubine, *not* the wife, of Constantius. But this is a questionable assumption, which appears to have arisen from a gratuitous interpretation by Zosimus [1] and Orosius [2] of some words used by Eutropius: *ex obscuriori matrimonio eius filius.*[3] But that phrase need signify no more than that Helena was of obscure and humble birth; and indeed St Ambrose describes her father as an innkeeper (*stabularius*). Surely too, by insisting on her divorce, Diocletian may be taken to have

[1] ii. 8. [2] vii. 25. [3] x. 2.

recognized her marriage. The date of her conversion to Christianity is open to dispute. It is usually said that she was received as a catechumen while her son was still a child, and streams of sentimentality have poured from the hagiographers, who picture the great Constantine learning of Christ and the true faith at his beloved mother's knee. Eusebius, however, assures us [1] that Helena herself was indebted to Constantine for her knowledge of Christianity. Be that as it may, we know that when Constantine became emperor he loaded his mother with the highest honours, conferring upon her the title Augusta and striking coins that bear her portrait. It is also certain that in 326 she made a pilgrimage to the Holy Land and with her son's help founded several churches. The well-known story that she discovered the Cross is not well documented until the late fourth century. It appears to have been unknown to the Pilgrim of Bordeaux (333), Eusebius and St Cyril of Jerusalem; the earliest reference occurs in a sermon of St Ambrose (395).

The date of Helena's death is uncertain. In medieval England legends arose representing her as daughter of a British prince; Geoffrey of Monmouth makes her a daughter of Coel, eponymous King of Colchester, and some say the 'Old King Cole' of the song! Such idle tales were due to the renown of Constantine, who trod a bloody but a splendid path from York to the Capitol, to the fields of Hadrianople and the heights of Chrysopolis.

In the year 306 the Emperor Constantius lay once again at Gessoriacum preparing to undertake a second British expedition, this time against the Picts, and he wrote to Galerius, now Augustus of the East, asking that his son be allowed to accompany him. Constantine had already brilliantly distinguished himself on active service in more than one campaign, and the high favour in which he stood both with the army and with the civilian population had aroused the suspicion and jealousy of Galerius. However, after much delay, permission for the journey was reluctantly granted, since refusal might have precipitated an armed conflict. Fearing a last-minute change of mind on the part of Galerius, Constantine left the palace of Nicomedia at dead of night and travelled with incredible speed, always apprehensive of pursuit by emissaries of Galerius or of interception by his father's Caesar, Flavius Severus, a creature of the eastern Emperor. He reached

[1] *Vit. Constant.* iii. 47.

Gessoriacum in safety when his father was on the point of embarkation.

After a brilliant victory over the Picts, in which his son took part, Constantius died at York, headquarters of the Sixth Legion, on 25th June 306, and Constantine was immediately proclaimed Augustus by the troops. Galerius would recognize him only as Caesar, and with authority only over the transalpine provinces. With that for the moment he had to be content.

During the seven months of Constantine's residence in Britain the Christians continued to live under the protection and goodwill extended to them by his father; and two other factors may have helped to confirm his belief in the wisdom no less than in the justice of such a policy. Not only had he witnessed with disgust the cruelties inflicted upon the Christians of Nicomedia during the first years of Diocletian's persecution,[1] but he also had reason to admire the Christian discipline, which inculcated public and private virtue as well as loyalty to the throne, a loyalty already inspired by common gratitude for the generosity with which his father had endeavoured to soften or to ignore the edicts of Diocletian.

But to an ambitious man such as Constantine, more important than the gratitude of the Christians would have been the loyalty of the army. To it he owed his title of Caesar, and to it he would have to look for any wider achievement that he might yet seek. We can hardly doubt therefore that during those seven months he visited the chief military centres, to see and to be seen by the troops. We can imagine him, for example, riding from York across the highlands of Britain to visit in state the fortress town of Chester, stronghold of the Twentieth Legion. There he would receive the acclaim of the garrison and gaze across the blue hills to the west, beyond which lay the mountains of Wales. Or we can imagine him travelling south to Caerleon to review the troops of the Second Legion. Away to the east lay the great port of Richborough, principal gateway of military supplies and reinforcements from the Continent. He would have remembered that here the troops of Claudius landed over two hundred years before; and he may have mused on the old Empire, which was governed by one man who wielded absolute power, sharing it with no one. From his later actions we know that Constantine cherished the ambition of rebuilding such

[1] *Oratio ad Sanctorum Coetum*, preserved by Eusebius.

an empire, with himself at the centre, sole and unchallenged ruler of the world.

Seven months after his father's death and his own accession to power, Constantine left Britain for Gaul, where he established his headquarters and began to plan the fulfilment of his dreams.

3

THE VISION OF CONSTANTINE

THERE is no need here to retell the complicated story of intrigue and murder, of alliances made and dissolved, of war and truce, of external pressures and internal fractures, which caused the breakdown of Diocletian's system of the four emperors, and which brought Constantine at long last from small beginnings to sole and undisputed mastery of the Roman world. Three episodes, however, deserve our attention. The first two are landmarks in the history of Christianity; the third, less dramatic, affords us our first unclouded view of the Church in Britain.

At Rome in 312 the usurper Maxentius, son of Diocletian's old colleague Maximian, had governed, or rather misgoverned, Italy and Africa for a period of six years, and laid claim to the entire half of the Western Empire. With him Constantine now prepared to dispute the issue in what he foresaw would be the decisive battle of his career. Victory crowned his arms at Saxa Rubra and the Milvian Bridge.

We are told by Lactantius,[1] writing about three years after the event, that during the night before the battle Constantine was ordered in a dream to mark the shields of his troops with the 'celestial sign of God' (i.e. the Cross); that he did as directed, and that his obedience was rewarded with the victory we have described. More than twenty years later, in his *Life of Constantine*,[2] Eusebius elaborated this story. According to him the Emperor, on one of his marches before he crossed the Alps, beheld a luminous figure of the Cross, standing above

[1] *De Mort. Persec.* 44. [2] i. 28–30.

the noonday sun and bearing the words, 'By this conquer'. This extraordinary phenomenon amazed the whole army, but Constantine's wonder was converted to belief by a dream on the following night. Christ appeared to him carrying the same Cross and told him to make a standard of like pattern with which he could march against his enemy with assurance of victory. Now Eusebius appears conscious that his story may be viewed with distrust by his readers.[1] Yet instead of supporting it with details of time and place, instead of collecting the testimony of those numerous men who must have been present when the miracle occurred, he relies merely upon a statement of the deceased Emperor who, he says, told him of the incident and backed his word with a solemn oath. These facts, together with the silence of the Fathers of the fourth and fifth centuries who so often celebrate the triumph of Constantine, entitle us to ask how genuine was the vision?

If we accept the extant *Life of Constantine* as an authentic work of Eusebius, and believe him to have related honestly what he had been told, it is clear that the Emperor was anxious to convince his contemporaries and posterity of the truth of the story and of the divine support his actions had received. But many historians have cast doubt upon his integrity and have suggested that Constantine was guided throughout by political motives.

There is incontrovertible evidence that both before and after his 'vision' Constantine was punctilious in the observance of pagan worship. He restored and enriched the temples of the pagan gods. His coins bear the images of Jupiter and Apollo, of Mars and Hercules; and one at least suggests that he allowed the formal apotheosis of his father. Following the example of Maximian, he at first acknowledged Hercules as patron of his reign; after 310, when he drove the ex-emperor to suicide, he began to invoke the Invincible Sun, *Sol Invictus*, a deity who was also at the heart of Mithraism. Finally, in 321, he published two edicts. The first enjoined official observance of Sunday[2] —*dies solis* (the day of the sun), a phrase which could not offend his pagan subjects. The second revived a pagan practice by providing for regular consultation of the Haruspices.[3]

[1] It does not occur in his *Ecclesiastical History*.

[2] *Cod. Theodos*. II. viii. 1.

[3] Ibid. XVI. x. i.

Nevertheless, whatever may have been his motives, or whatever may have been the degree of his sincerity, it is evident that from 312, the year of his vision and six years from his taking power in Britain, Constantine identified the Christian cause with his own and saw himself as the chosen instrument of the Christian God. That fact alone proclaims the Church as already a vital and irresistible force on the threshold of a new age.

4

THE EDICT OF MILAN AND THE SYNOD OF ARLES

AMONG the first official acts of Constantine after his victory was the restoration to the churches in Africa of the property which had been confiscated during the persecutions. Although the written evidence we possess refers only to Africa, there can be little doubt that the same was done elsewhere. We may therefore take it that in Britain the Christian communities received the joyful news during the winter of 312. With their property returned, they could now afford to rebuild those of their churches which, in spite of the protection afforded by Constantius, were destroyed in the unhappy days of Diocletian's persecution. This was possibly the time, about which Gildas wrote, when churches were being rebuilt and restored everywhere. With the martyrdom of St Alban still fresh in men's minds, it may have been now that the first church was built on the place of his martyrdom, where later the cathedral was to stand. Indeed Bede tells us that the church at Verulamium was built when peaceful times were restored for the Christians, which phrase might well refer to this act of Constantine.

Added to this joy, which they shared with their co-religionists throughout the Empire, the Christians in Britain must have felt a special thrill of pride that it was Constantine (an emperor whose imperial origins lay in the island) who was giving this new freedom and happiness to the Church.

In 313 there was published the celebrated Edict of Milan,[1] signed jointly by Constantine and Licinius, ruler of the Illyrian and Eastern provinces. The text is preserved in Eusebius's *Life of Constantine*, and here are the words that meant the dawn of a new era for Christians everywhere:

> We grant full liberty to Christians and to everyone, that they may follow what religion is agreeable to them. . . . Each Christian may individually, freely and unhindered, pursue such observance of his religion as he wills. . . . Also the places where Christians were wont formerly to assemble, if these have been purchased by others, must be restored to the Christians without money or other compensation. . . . The Christians possessed not only meeting houses and private dwellings but also other property held by their body, that is their communities. Such property we command to be restored without delay or argument.

Christianity, after more than two hundred and fifty years of struggle, was now a legal religion throughout the Empire, in all the lands both of the East and of the West. But the struggles of the past had left their mark upon the Church. In Africa, for example, there was argument as to whether Caecilian, who was said to have surrendered copies of the Holy Scriptures to be burned during the troubles, could properly be appointed Bishop of Carthage. Constantine supported Caecilian, but there was great opposition. This was led by Donatus, the rival bishop. In 314, only a year after the edict, a synod was convened at Arles in France to consider the dispute.[2] This is a remarkable indication of how swiftly, a bare two years after the Vision of Constantine, the Church saw itself as an imperial institution, calling upon bishops in western Europe to study and to pronounce upon the facts of a dispute in North Africa.

The thirty-three bishops who assembled at Arles condemned the followers of Donatus as heretics, and gave their support to Constantine's candidate Caecilian.

[1] Lactantius, *De Mort. Persec.* 48; Eusebius, *Hist. Eccl.*

[2] It was the first general assembly of the Western Church. Its twenty-two canons are extant.

The most important fact about this council from our point of view was that among the bishops attending it were three from Britain. In the Corbie Codex, dating from the sixth or seventh century, their names are listed: *Eborius de Civitate Eboracensi, Restitutus de Civitate Londiniensi, Adelphius de Civitate colonia Londinensium.*

The second is the only name which the manuscript appears to give correctly: Restitutus, from the City of London. The first names the see correctly, the City of York. The Latin name for York was *Eboracum*, and the Archbishop of York signs himself as ✠ Ebor to this day. The name *Eborius* is almost certainly a repetition of the name of the see; very likely the original compiler did not know this prelate's real name, so took the signature for the name. What was the see of Adelphius, the third bishop? *Colonia Londinensium* is obviously an error in the text. It cannot refer to London, which was not a *colonia* (a settlement of ex-servicemen), and which in any case has already been listed with its bishop, Restitutus. It has been suggested with much probability that the words are a blundered version of *colonia Camulodunensium* [1] and that Adelphius was Bishop of Colchester. That town was indeed a *colonia*, and was the first such settlement to be established in Britain (A.D. 50). Moreover it was in Colchester that the first temple to the divinity of the Emperor had been built at the time of the Claudian conquest, and the place had therefore been an important religious centre from the earliest times. Ian Richmond [2] suggested that the Bishop of Colchester was primate of Britain. He certainly had a position of special importance, for, alone of the three bishops from Britain, he was accompanied to Arles by two attendants—a priest and a deacon.

The summoning to Arles of the bishops of London, York and perhaps Colchester has interesting implications. First, it suggests that those sees were considered to be of sufficient importance for their incumbents to be invited to assist in the deliberations. This in turn suggests that the sees were of respectable age and had probably existed during the third century. The record certainly entitles us to believe that there was probably an organized Christian community extant in York when Constantius died there in 306, and when Constantine

[1] J. M. C. Toynbee, 'Christianity in Roman Britain', *Journal of the British Archaeological Association*, vol. xvi, 1953.

[2] *Arch. Journ.* ciii (1947), page 64.

was in that city. Next, the conference shows that the most important cities of Britain contained well-organized Christian communities in the early fourth century and that accordingly these communities were probably flourishing in the third. Finally, the conference shows the Christians in Britain as well known to, and in regular contact with, their fellow Christians on the Continent. The years of separation under Carausius and Allectus had not permanently divided Britain from the affairs of the Empire.

These contacts were to continue throughout the period of Roman rule and indeed beyond it.

In 325 the Church in Britain accepted the rulings given by the council which Constantine had summoned at Nicaea.[1] It is not known whether Britain was represented at the Council of Sardica in 343, but its decrees were accepted by the British Churches.[2] Next, at least three British bishops, their expenses provided for out of the imperial treasury, attended the Council of Rimini in 360.[3]

Britain was now very much a part of the Christian community of the Empire. In her cities, from the south-east to the far north, bishops ordered their flocks and watched over the welfare of men's souls. Through their bishops, Christians in the island were in contact with distant lands and with the decisions and decrees of Constantine, servant of the servants of Christ, whose first step towards power had been taken in Britain.

For some ten years Constantine shared power with Licinius. But in 323 Licinius was defeated by his colleague and retired into private life. Shortly afterwards he was put to death. Constantine's destiny was now fulfilled. Once more, as in the days of Augustus and his successors, the Empire was ruled by one man. Constantine, who had first been acclaimed by the army in Britain, was now supreme and undisputed ruler of the whole Roman world.

[1] Athanasius, *Ad Jovian. imp.*
[2] Athanasius, *Apol. con. Arian.*
[3] Sulpicius Severus, *Hist. Sacra*, xi. 41.

5

CHURCHES IN BRITAIN

THROUGH the words of Gildas and the brief record of the Synod of Arles we catch a glimpse of the churches and cathedral churches of Britain in the reign of Constantine. The glimpse we have is shadowy, and no physical traces remain, or have yet been discovered, of the cathedrals of the three bishops. Nor do we know where stood the many churches which Gildas tells us were built or renovated after Constantine had given peace and liberty to the faith.

Nevertheless archaeologists have revealed one or two places that may have been built for Christian worship and which give a further dimension to the literary references.

The city of *Calleva Atrebatum* (modern Silchester), once the proud walled capital of one of the regions of Britain, is now a level stretch of farmland. The grey walls still stand, but they no longer enclose houses, shops and temples. Within the walls there lie open fields where corn and grasses grow. At ploughing time a scattering of red brick fragments among the furrows is the only sign left that here was once a town. In 1892 parts of Calleva were excavated, and there came to light a small building that is generally accepted as having been a Christian church on the score of its very church-like ground plan, although no Christian paintings or objects have come to light in it. It is 43 feet long (east to west) and almost 33 feet wide (north to south). There is a central nave, just under ten feet wide. At the western end of the nave there is a semicircular apse, and on either side are two small square rooms which are, as it were, rudimentary transepts. They jut out, to north and south, beyond the narrow aisles on either side of the nave. The slight protrusion of these transepts, together with the semicircular apse, give the building a cruciform ground plan. This in itself is not conclusive evidence that it was a Christian church. Shrines of the mystery cults had similar plans. But the theory that the building was a place of Christian worship is a likely one.

At the western end of the nave, and lying just outside the curved floor of the apse, there is a small mosaic pavement about four feet square. It consists of an inner square of black-and-white chequer pattern, surrounded by a border of larger black and white squares and then by a black border. This mosaic 'carpet' is quite unworn, and it would therefore appear that something stood upon it permanently, so protecting it from the tread of either priest or worshippers. Its prominent position is such as to suggest very strongly that the object which stood upon it was an altar. For the mosaic to have remained visible (and we cannot imagine that it would have been carefully positioned and constructed merely to lie hidden), we must assume that the altar was originally a table beneath which the chequer pattern could be seen. Later, perhaps, the first wooden table (from which no doubt the communicants took their bread and wine) was replaced by a stone structure. For the excavators reported that they found traces of pink cement on the surface of the mosaic.

The floor of the nave was made up of plain red mosaic, with no pattern or design. This floor has one puzzling feature. When it was excavated it showed considerable signs of wear just to the east of the mosaic 'carpet', that is to say on the side facing the nave and the congregation. It has been argued that this wear was caused by the priest and that therefore he must have celebrated Mass facing the altar to the west, and with his back to the congregation. While this is not impossible it is somewhat unlikely. Where a church had a western apse the priest would normally stand behind the altar, facing the east, and looking towards the worshippers gathered in the nave. It has been suggested that perhaps the custom of facing east for the Mass had not yet reached Britain. There is, however, a simple alternative explanation for the worn floor in front of the altar. After the bread and wine had been blessed, members of the congregation would have come up to the altar from their seats in the nave to receive Holy Communion. They would have stood at the front of the altar, perhaps two or three at a time, facing the priest across it. Many would have been in their workaday clothes, with heavily studded boots. Surely it is the footsteps of the many worshippers rather than the feet of the one priest which, through the years of the building's life, wore away the pavement and scuffed away the hard brick squares of the floor.

The wear tells us another story. It suggests that Christian worship may have continued here long after the prosperity of the town had faded. Otherwise such a sacred place would surely have been repaired, and the floor in front of the altar put to rights. So we have the picture of long years of use, into the dark days when good order was withering and when the Christian community of Calleva, once rich enough to erect its own church, could no longer afford even the simplest of repairs. We have a picture of the grandsons and grand-daughters of the founders walking through the now shabby streets to join in worship in the now shabby church. The worn floor, the loose tesserae of the red mosaic, were no doubt matched by a general decay of the building. Damp walls, peeling plaster and shabby doors no doubt met the eyes of the communicants when they were raised from prayer. But these things probably made little impression, for they were signs of the general decay and deterioration throughout the town, with which all were familiar.

To the east of the building there was discovered a foundation, made of cement and tiles, some four feet square. Upon this there possibly stood a font for baptism.

After the 1892 excavation, the whole site was filled in, and the remains of the building once more lay hidden beneath the earth. They have since been re-excavated, with more modern methods and techniques, but the results have not so far been published. Meantime it is believed that the little church was built sometime around 300, for the chequered mosaic is very similar to one found at St Albans and dated to that period. So in the reign of Constantine the Christians of Calleva worshipped in their little church where now the dry corn stubble and the long grasses in their seasons cover the ruins, and the memory of those humble folk is almost departed.

From its nature we surmise that this was a place of public worship. We also have evidence of Christianity in the beautifully appointed and decorated homes of the rich. At Lullingstone in Kent there has been excavated a large and magnificent villa, obviously the home of an extremely wealthy family. Some of the rooms on the ground floor had, about the middle of the fourth century, richly painted walls. The plaster had crumbled and fallen to the ground. The fragments were carefully collected when the building was excavated, and have been fitted together, so that large portions of the original wall paintings have been restored. The result is one of quite startling magnificence.

One of the rooms at the northern end of the villa had on its western wall a painting of seven columns supporting a roof. Between each pair of columns was a human figure rather more than half life-size, and of these some parts remain. Their garments are of fourth-century fashion, having circular decorations and pearl-edged stripes woven into or embroidered upon them and the long sleeves fit tightly to the wrists. Two of the heads survive, and these have red hair and bright eyes.

Behind one of the figures hangs a curtain, suspended from a rod just behind the head. Such curtains were often used by the Romans, both pagan and Christian, to indicate that the person depicted was dead, and it may well be that the same applied here. Some of the figures are shown with their arms extending laterally across the pillars at their sides, with their hands open. This, originally a pagan attitude of prayer, is typical of early Christian art, and is to be seen both in the catacombs and on many Christian sarcophagi of the third and fourth centuries.

In paintings of this date the attitude of the figures alone indicates, therefore, that the room may have been used as a place of Christian worship, and Professor Toynbee records that it was this that immediately suggested to her a Christian *milieu* for the frescoes. Her deduction received striking corroboration when in 1952 further plaster fragments were reassembled and two large-scale representations of the sacred monogram, Chi-Rho, were revealed. One came from the same room as the figures. Painted in bright red on a white background, it is surrounded by a wreath of buds and leaves. It was flanked by two pillars. The second monogram, also painted in red on a white background, and also surrounded by a wreath, came from a smaller adjoining room. To the right of the monogram there are still to be seen fragments of the letter omega. The letter alpha must have been painted on the left: 'I am the Alpha and the Omega. . . '.

Indisputably, therefore, the villa at Lullingstone was owned by Christians and the painted room was probably a place of Christian worship, but whether the rooms were public church or private chapel must remain in some doubt. Perhaps during its history it served both purposes. The painted figures, one of whom at least appears to have died before the picture was made, might well be portraits of members of the owner's family—those still living and those who lay awaiting their certain resurrection. This suggests that the two rooms were originally an oratory where the family and their servants gathered together for prayer. Perhaps no priest presided, but the head of the house, like the *paterfamilias* of pagan days, led his household in prayer and in the singing of hymns. Later, perhaps, the rooms became the centre for a wider circle of worshippers, drawn from the neighbouring countryside and from the farms and cottages close by. There is some evidence for this kind of development. For the door leading from these rooms to the rest of the villa was blocked up and a new door, leading directly from the painted rooms to the countryside outside, was opened up some time during the fourth century. This alteration separated the two painted rooms, and the small room adjoining, from the rest of the house, and gave them an isolated significance that is no longer consistent with their having been merely the household chapel. At the time when the work was done, it would appear that the rooms were no longer regarded as part of the house. Perhaps they had now become a public church to which came all the local Christians, who worshipped God in the richly decorated rooms and who looked upon the wealthy owner as their patron and friend.

Of other physical traces of church or chapel during this period there are none. However, there is some material evidence that many churches, built long after the Roman period, were erected on the site of earlier Roman buildings. The Saxons did not normally build on the site of Roman villas or towns. Indeed they usually avoided doing so. St Albans is a typical example; there the Saxon town was built on the hillside at some distance from the deserted Roman shops, temples and houses, which were allowed to fall into ruin. Villas were left to crumble to dust, and the Saxon farmer built his timber house well away from these eerie reminders of a past age. Hence where we find a church built over a former Roman building we are entitled to wonder whether there was some special reason. For example, if the Roman building had itself been a church, then the Saxons, after their conversion, might well have chosen the spot out of piety. In the same way, if a deserted villa still bore signs of Christian worship or occupation, piety again might have prompted the Saxons to build their new church upon the old foundation.

Up and down the country there are many churches within which are displayed fragments of Roman pottery that have been dug up in the churchyard and suggesting that the church stands on the site of an earlier Roman building. In the fabric of St Mary's Church at Prittlewell, in Essex, are numerous Roman bricks. The same is true of the church at Minster in the same county. Professor Toynbee records the Roman villa at Widford in Oxfordshire, discovered beneath St Oswald's Church; the Roman building beneath the church of St Mary at Lyminge in Kent; and Roman houses beneath the churches of West Mersea and Stansted Mountfichet in Essex, of Canwick in Lincolnshire, and under Southwell Minster, Canterbury Cathedral and All-Hallows-by-the-Tower in the City of London. Part of the church of St Bride's, Fleet Street, is composed of Roman materials, and below it have been discovered Roman walls and a tessellated pavement. There are many examples of villas in or near village churchyards.

It may be, of course, that these spots were chosen for no more dramatic a reason than that the older buildings provided a source of supply of stone, brick and other material. But, with such exceptions as St Albans Cathedral, which is built almost entirely of Roman bricks taken from the ruins of Verulamium, the proportion of reused building material is too small to suggest that it alone was the motive. This, coupled with the Saxons' usual avoidance of Roman sites, and the great number of churches of the kind mentioned, suggests that the existence of older Christian sites is the more likely reason for the selection of these spots by the Saxons for their churches.

Thus many of the churches, in town and village alike, are probably the heirs of buildings now vanished, or whose foundations lie hidden, where Christians worshipped in the reign of Constantine and in the years that followed.

6

CHRISTIAN VILLAS

ARCHAEOLOGY has revealed to us several private homes in Britain which were occupied by Christians during the fourth century and which they decorated with symbols of their faith. Three of these villas bear the Chi-Rho monogram as part of their permanent decoration.

The first of them to be unearthed was at Frampton in western Dorset. This was excavated in the late eighteenth century. Three of the rooms had elaborately decorated mosaic floors, which are all now lost. Fortunately good coloured drawings made at the time of discovery survive. The chief room was in two parts: the floor of the smaller portion consisted of a central square flanked by two oblong panels; the larger section, which was a square, was linked to the smaller by a mosaic panel between two projecting side walls. In the larger portion there was a central mosaic circle surrounded by four half-circles. One side of the square terminated in an apse and there was a large Chi-Rho monogram worked in the centre of the floral scroll on the chord of this apse.

In the centre circle there is a mounted figure pursuing and spearing a beast. The rider may be a depiction of the pagan hero Bellerophon slaying the Chimaera. This is by no means certain, for the drawing shows no trace of any goat's head growing out of the beast's neck, as would be the case with the Chimaera. On the other hand the drawing seems to show that the horse had wings, and this would suggest that the steed was Pegasus, the flying horse that was the traditional mount of Bellerophon. In fact a reconstruction of the group as Bellerophon with the Chimaera fits the space very satisfactorily.

The presence of the Chi-Rho monogram is positive evidence that the villa was owned by a Christian family. The juxtaposition of the mounted figure, be he simple huntsman or the hero Bellerophon, indicates that Christianity had not entirely obliterated the taste for secular or even traditionally pagan themes for decoration, drawn from classical mythology. Even in pagan times such depictions of mythical beasts and characters had often been used allegorically. As we shall see, the Christians may have continued to use these themes, and to use them in the same way.

The next villa to be discovered with Christian emblems was that at Lullingstone, mentioned in the last chapter and excavated initially in 1949, with the two Chi-Rho monograms painted on the walls of two of the ground-floor rooms. Here also is to be found the juxtaposition of Christian emblem and pagan hero, for on the mosaic floor of the adjoining room (the triclinium) there is shown the undoubted figure of Bellerophon slaying his adversary the Chimaera (part lion, part goat and part serpent) with a downward thrust of his spear. It is a particularly fine piece of work. The colours are gay, and the mosaic squares making up the horse's reins consist of small pieces of Samian pottery, the bright red glazed earthenware that was so esteemed by the Romans. In the same room there is a couplet, the letters carefully built up of the tiny mosaic squares, alluding to the classical poet Virgil. It is placed under a depiction of Europa.

The third discovery is perhaps the most dramatic of all. On the western portion of the mosaic floor of a large room in a villa at Hinton St Mary in Somerset (excavated in 1963) the Chi-Rho monogram appears in the central medallion, behind the head of a man facing east, which is almost certainly a portrait of Christ. The face is clean-shaven with deep-set and commanding eyes. His hair is combed forward over the brow and falls in locks on either side of the powerful neck. It shows us clearly what must have been the traditional image of Christ among His followers in fourth-century Britain. The face is grave, calm and powerful, with an imperious rather than a gentle appearance. It is the face of the Ruler of the world, one whom the Emperor himself was proud to serve.

As at Frampton, the room is divided into two parts. Here the floor of the smaller and western part contains a large circular mosaic medallion, over seven feet in diameter, upon which again appears, facing west, the figure of Bellerophon slaying the Chimaera. The rider's head and most of his body have vanished. But the monster is complete. Over it leaps the horse, and Bellerophon is thrusting his spear downwards into the goat's head in the centre of the monster's back.

Surely it is significant that Bellerophon appears in two of the three villas so far discovered with the Chi-Rho monogram, and that a figure very like Bellerophon's appears in the third. The question must be asked whether this pagan hero had been adopted by the Christians of Britain as a suitable symbol for their religious ideas.

We must remember that educated Christians of this period would have been brought up on the traditional classical literature and mythology. They would not have seen Christianity as shutting them off from their older heritage. The allusion to Virgil inscribed under the Europa mosaic in the apse of the triclinium of the Lullingstone villa is proof of this. They would have known in detail the story of Bellerophon, son of the King of Corinth. His name was Hipponoüs, but he became known as Bellerophon, the slayer of Belerus. To be purified from blood-guilt he fled to Proetus, King of Argos. The latter's wife fell in love with him and, when he refused her advances, accused him to her husband of having attempted to ravish her. Proetus believed this story and sent Bellerophon to Iobates, King of Lycia, with a sealed letter. Iobates received Bellerophon kindly, not revealing that the letter contained a request to kill him. He set him the task of destroying the Chimaera, a three-headed monster, part lion, part goat and part dragon, quite sure that the hero would be slain in the enterprise. But Bellerophon obtained from Athene the winged horse Pegasus, mounted it and slew the Chimaera. Although in some versions of the story he was said to have killed the monster with his arrows, he came to be depicted as a spearman, trampling the dragon-like monster beneath his horse's hooves, and stabbing downwards with his spear.

Professor Toynbee suggests that 'Bellerophon slaying the Chimaera would be an allegory of the overcoming of death and evil, a christianized pagan allegory drawn from that traditional storehouse of Graeco-Roman mythology that was the fourth-century Christian's cultural heritage'. [1] There can be little doubt that this is correct. The precise meaning of the allegory cannot now be determined. Whether it represented the conquest of death by faith, or of unrighteousness by righteousness, or of the devil and his works by the new religion, is no longer clear. It is enough to take it as a generalized representation of the triumph of things good over things evil, adopted by Christians in Britain as a symbol of their faith.

If this is so, then we must assume that there were numerous other examples of such allegorical uses of pagan myths by Christians in addition to those that have by chance come to light. It is inconceivable that we have, by the merest hazard, unearthed every example. It has already been noted that, after the end of the Roman power in Britain, and after the coming of the Saxons, the latter did not occupy the deserted Roman villas or build their own houses upon the same sites. Thus by the time the Saxons themselves were converted to Christianity (during the early seventh century) many of the empty villas, though derelict and decaying, would have remained undisturbed and in a fair state of preservation. We can imagine these later and now Christian Saxons, less superstitious than their pagan grandfathers, examining the

[1] *Journal of Roman Studies*, vol. liv, 1964.

old buildings, and looking upon them with wonder rather than with fear. We know from Bede that they now restored and reoccupied former Romano-British churches that had long lain neglected. In the same way they would have looked with pious curiosity upon those villas that showed signs of earlier Christian occupation. Had they seen in them, as seems highly probable from the evidence we have examined, many representations of Bellerophon slaying the monster, they would have surely puzzled out some explanation to bring it within the Christian story. No one then remembered, or indeed had ever known, the stories of classical mythology. None of the Saxons, nor possibly even of those Christians who had come from Rome, would have known the story of Bellerophon, Prince of Corinth. An interpretation had to be found that lay within their knowledge. What angel was this, or what saint? And over what strange and hideous monster was this Christian champion riding in triumph? Perhaps it was a monk, more learned than his fellows, who remembered George of Cappadocia, the cavalry soldier who was also a Christian saint. Perhaps St George's name became attached to the recurrent image of Bellerophon, and grew to be a symbol of Christianity in the minds of the English. Certainly the later drawings of St George show a striking likeness to the Bellerophon of the Christian villas and certainly there must be some very special reason why a rather obscure saint from an unknown land of the Near East should have later become the patron saint of England, rather than one of the island's own martyrs.

7

OTHER CHRISTIAN OBJECTS

IN ADDITION to the evidence concerning the three individual homes that were at some time owned by Christian families, archaeology also offers testimony that Christians dwelt in many of the towns of Britain during the fourth century.

Richborough Castle in Kent is all that remains of *Portus Rutupiae*, once the main port of Roman Britain. On three sides the grey walls still stand. On the fourth the cliff has fallen away, taking the wall with it. Here once stood the monument commemorating Rome's conquest of the island; here ships from the Continent came to harbour, and here more than one emperor must have landed when visiting the island province. It was the main strongpoint of the south-eastern defences, and a main link in Rome's system of communications.

In the fourth report on the excavations at Richborough, published in 1949, J. P. Bushe-Fox records the finding of a thin bronze medallion. It is embossed with the bust of a man encircled with a laurel wreath. Near his hand is a Chi-Rho monogram, to which he seems to be pointing. He is clean-shaven, and a cloak is flung over his shoulders.

Mattingly has pointed out that the face is very like that of the Emperor Magnentius as depicted on his coins. The identification seems probable, for, likeness apart, many of his coins did bear Christian symbols and the Chi-Rho monogram might well have been embodied in the design of a portrait medallion. Magnentius reigned from 350 to 353. If the medallion dates from his reign it is good evidence for Christians in *Portus Rutupiae* during the middle of the fourth century.

During the first excavation of Richborough (reported in 1923) Bushe-Fox records the find of another object that could be Christian. This is a small bone plaque inscribed with a letter S and the word VIVAS. The S is obviously the last letter of a masculine name; VIVAS means 'may you live' and could be part of the Christian formula VIVAS IN DEO—'May you live in God!' Here again there may be evidence for Christians dwelling in the busy port.

We have already seen that there was probably a church at *Calleva Atrebatum*, modern Silchester. On the site of the same town there was found a fragment of a glass drinking vessel, engraved with the Christian symbols of a fish and a palm branch.[1] This, even if no church building had come to light, would suggest that Christians lived in the city, and that they liked to have the symbols of their faith displayed upon objects of daily use. But it must be remembered that these two symbols were also pagan ones, so that this evidence is not conclusive.

A hundred years ago, before the site was excavated, there was also found at Silchester a lead seal stamped on both sides with the Chi-Rho

[1] *Archaeologia*, cviii, 1902.

monogram together with the letters alpha and omega. This tells us a little more about the Christians in *Calleva*, for it indicates that some at least of them were fairly wealthy. A seal of this kind would have been used on goods or property, and would have been owned by a well-to-do personage or even by the church itself.

There is also a gold finger ring found at or near Silchester. It has a rectangular bezel upon which is engraved a woman's head, with the name VENUS inscribed beside it. The ring must therefore have been of pagan origin; but it later became the property of a Christian. For round the ring itself is engraved (with two spelling errors) SENICIANE VIVAS IN DEO—'Senicianus, may you live in God!' The inscription suggests that the ring was a present to Senicianus, himself a Christian, from a Christian friend.

The modern city of Canterbury stands on the site of the Roman city of *Durovernum*. Here again there is fairly abundant archaeological evidence for Christianity during this period. Just outside the town there was found in 1927 an almost complete bowl of the bright red ware known as Samian. It was made some time late in the second century, and had been treasured and carefully preserved until the late 300's. On its base is scratched the Chi-Rho monogram. This certainly proves Christian ownership. But whether the bowl was simply the prized possession of a Christian, or whether it was actually used in formal ceremony—perhaps as a Communion cup—we shall never know.

In 1965 [1] a small hoard of silver and gold objects was found within the town of Canterbury itself. There was a fine gold ring and a gold hook and eye. There was also a silver pin and no fewer than eleven silver spoons, together with two ingots of silver and a small implement of the same metal. One of the spoons, which is just over four inches long and which has a finely worked handle in the shape of a bird's head, bears the Chi-Rho monogram in the centre of the bowl. The implement consists of a handle of square section, twisted in a kind of barley-sugar fashion. At one end there is a tiny spoon. At the other there is a round disk upon which is a neatly executed the Chi-Rho monogram, partly punched and partly engraved. From the disk there springs a curved prong. Together with these objects there was found a number of coins dating from 354 to 423. Here again is evidence not merely of

[1] Kenneth Painter, *Journal of the British Archaeological Association*, vol. xxviii.

Christians in one of the cities of Britain, but of Christians who possessed considerable wealth. The spoon is a very beautiful object and must have been expensive. The implement, whatever its use may have been, is also a fine example of the silversmith's art and must have been the property of a wealthy person.

That London had a bishop in 314 we have already seen. There must therefore have been a considerable number of Christians dwelling there. But the archaeological evidence is scant in the extreme. A bowl in the London Museum, found at Copthall Court, has the Chi-Rho monogram very roughly scratched on the base. This single relic shows how slight is the chance of the survival of fragile everyday objects, and underlines the significance of the physical evidence, small though it may seem, which has in fact endured and come down to us.

Other sites up and down Britain have contributed their scraps of information. In the Yorkshire Museum are three groups of fretted bone letters, the decoration of some object that has perished, which read S[OR]OR AVE VIVAS IN DEO—'Hail, sister! May you live in God!' They were found in a stone coffin in which a woman lay buried with her jewellery and a few fine glass vessels.

From Margate comes a terra-cotta lamp, with the Chi-Rho symbol moulded upon it. In Exeter was found a fragment of black pottery with the sacred monogram scratched on its surface. From Brancaster in Norfolk, which was once a Roman fort guarding the east coast of Britain, comes a signet ring. The seal shows two heads and the words VIVAS IN DEO—'May you live in God!'

The objects from such military centres as Richborough, York and Brancaster are of particular interest. For they show, as we would expect after the liberation of the Church by Constantine, that there were Christians in the army as well as among the civilian population.

There is also evidence for Christianity in the countryside. Near Mildenhall in Suffolk, in a field on the edge of the fens, lie the remains of a fourth-century Roman building. In 1942 a great hoard of silverware was unearthed by the plough some thirty yards from this building. The main item was a massive silver dish, almost two feet across and weighing over eighteen pounds. In relief upon the gleaming silver there is a lively scene showing Bacchus the wine god triumphing over a tipsy and staggering Hercules. God and hero alike are naked, as are the prancing satyrs and the great god Pan who dances among the revellers.

Besides this splendid piece there are other smaller dishes, and also bowls, plates and goblets—all in fine silver. Satyrs and maenads dance on the plates, as does Pan, playing his pipes. There are also six fine spoons, three of which were definitely used by Christians, for the bowl of each is inscribed with the sacred monogram of Christ, set between the letters alpha and omega.

The pieces were evidently all buried together and the Christian who had owned the spoons may therefore also have owned the great dish and the rest of the items. It does not follow that this was the case, since 'Christian' spoons may have found their way into the treasure of a tolerant non-Christian, but, if he was a Christian, the richness of the hoard suggests that he was one who possessed influence and power. When the pagan barbarians were invading Britain during the last days of Roman rule, perhaps he personally supervised the hiding away of his wealth hoping that, when peace was restored, they would be restored to him. In fact it was to be some sixteen hundred years afterwards when the naked gods and the Christian inscriptions were again to see the sunlight.[1]

At the large and prosperous villa at Chedworth in Gloucestershire there is a slab of stone engraved with the sacred monogram. Eight ingots of pewter were found in the Thames between Battersea and Wandsworth; each bears the name Syagrius and a medallion with the Chi-Rho. Some have the alpha and omega stamped upon them, others the words SPES IN DEO—'In God is hope'.

At Icklingham in Suffolk there is the site of a Roman villa. In 1939 there was discovered about 150 yards from the villa a large circular lead vessel now in the British Museum. It is about 2 ft 8 in. in diameter and about 13 in. deep. Of excellent workmanship, it is made of three pieces of lead sheet. One circular piece forms the base and two rectangular pieces, joined together, form the sides. Round the rim there is a moulding of cable pattern. In addition there is a series of vertical ribs with a zigzag decoration, dividing the sides into ten panels. These ribs seem to imitate linen straps, and the whole vessel seems to simulate, in lead, a large leather or cloth water-container supported within a rope and webbing frame. The front panel of the vessel bears a large Chi-Rho monogram with the alpha and omega. The corresponding panel at the back bears the monogram alone.[2]

[1] J. W. Brailsford, *The Mildenhall Treasure*, British Museum.
[2] *Journal of Roman Studies*, xxxiii (1943), p. 80.

This vessel may have been used in baptism and is usually described as a font. If so it is the earliest example in Britain. There can be no certainty on this point, but what is certain is that this costly article was owned by a Christian, and it is good evidence for the existence of yet another wealthy Christian family in Roman Britain.

In or about 1910 a collection of pewter vessels was found on the site of Ampleforth villa in the parish of Appleshaw, near Andover, in Hampshire.[1] Among the articles (which are now in the British Museum) there is a dish which has the Chi-Rho monogram scratched upon it. The vessels were all found together and they had evidently been concealed for safety. The monogram on the dish is evidence again of Christian occupation of a Roman villa. Among the other articles in the collection is a chalice-like cup. Such a cup, found in association with the dish bearing the sacred monogram, may itself have had a special purpose. It is tempting to see both the cup and the dish as vessels used in the Communion service. But we cannot assume that these vessels were so used. All we can say is that they had some special value to their owner, and were carefully hidden away during some time of danger. This may well have been during the fourth or fifth century, when pagan armies were attacking the island. Perhaps the owners were anxious that these vessels should not be desecrated by heathen hands and, even in their haste and peril, found time to hide them safely away.

The general picture that emerges from all the archaeological evidence is of Christianity spread widely through the island—in the major cities, in military centres, in great country houses and in humbler villages. There were Christians among all classes; there were rich owners of well-appointed villas, merchants and the owners of metal factories; men wealthy enough to wear golden rings; soldiers and legionaries in the garrison towns; rich men with silver vessels, the less wealthy with their pewter dishes, and the poorer folk who were content to scratch the holy monogram upon pieces of rough pottery.

By the middle of the fourth century, some two hundred and fifty years before ever Augustine set foot in Kent, Britain was well on the way to being a Christian island.[2]

[1] J. P. Freeman, *Field Archaeology as illustrated in Hampshire*, 1915.

[2] The material for this chapter is largely drawn from Professor J. M. C. Toynbee's article on Christianity in Roman Britain, *Journal of the British Archaeological Association*, vol. xvi, 1953.

8

THE SETBACK

THE fourth century, as we have seen from all the evidence, was a period when the Church prospered and spread throughout Britain. Constantine, liberator of the Church and devoted supporter of Christianity, fell ill shortly after Easter in the year 337. Although it was now a quarter of a century since he had first supported the Christian religion, and although during the whole of that time he had devoted himself to the wellbeing and organization of the Church, proudly seeing himself as the servant of God, he had not been baptized or even received imposition of hands as a catechumen. But now, during his last illness, he was baptized by Eusebius, Bishop of Nicomedia.[1] He died shortly afterwards, and when the news reached Britain the Christians there, in cathedral city, in garrison town and in country home, must have felt a very special sense of bereavement. He would have been mourned by Christians all over the Empire, but in Britain they remembered that this great emperor, benefactor of the Church and zealous servant of God, had the closest links with their own island.

For three months after his death the imperial throne was vacant. In September, after a mutiny of the army in Constantinople, the three sons of Constantine declared themselves emperors. Constantine, the eldest, received Britain, Gaul, Spain and part of North Africa as his dominions. London was among the mints where his coins were struck (frequently bearing the Chi-Rho monogram), and Christian worship in Britain no doubt continued prosperous during his reign. Constantius, the second son, took the East; Constans, the youngest, took Dacia, Macedonia, Pannonia, Italy and parts of North Africa. Constantius alone held his dominions securely, both his brothers being displaced by usurpers. But through all the political turmoil Christianity remained undisturbed.

Like his father before him, Constantius busied himself about Church

[1] He must be carefully distinguished from the historian, Eusebius of Ceasarea.

affairs. He summoned a Council of Bishops at Arles in 354 and another at Milan in the following year, with the aim of removing divisions in the Church and of bringing about a unity of faith and worship. In 360 a very large council was held at Rimini with over four hundred bishops attending. At least three of them, as noticed above, had come from Britain. Four years earlier Constantius had lightened the burden of taxation for some of the poorer clergy, and those in Britain must have felt the benefit of this measure.

In 355 he appointed as Caesar his cousin Julian, a young man in his twenties and a nephew of Constantine the Great. Julian had grown up a little apart from his imperial cousins, with no expectation of power, and had endured a wretched and lonely childhood. His father and elder brother were both killed during the mutiny of the army at Constantinople after Constantine's death. As a young man therefore he had tasted some of the bitterness of high politics, and had no doubt grown somewhat cynical about the glories and pomp of state.

Born at, or in the neighbourhood of, Constantinople,[1] he has himself left an account of his education.[2] At the age of seven he was given as tutor a eunuch named Mardonius, who was a lover of Greek philosophy and of the old pagan mythology. The loneliness of his life threw Julian very much upon his own resources and he lived much in the past, loving the old tales and fables and finding them far more to his liking than the formal instruction in the arid subtleties of Christian theology which he also received. But it was not only the heroes of a past age whom he grew to love—Achilles, Agamemnon and the rest. He became also passionately interested in Greek philosophy and the mystical explanations which philosophers had given to the ancient myths. In one of his letters, written years later to two of his fellow students,[3] he bids them not to despise the lighter side of literature nor to neglect the study of poetry. But he commends most of all the teachings of Plato and Aristotle. Typical of his interest in the past was his initiation into the Eleusinian mysteries, an ancient cult of the earth goddess Demeter.

This was the man who suddenly and unexpectedly was raised to the position of Caesar in 355 by Constantius, his Christian cousin. He threw himself with enthusiasm and efficiency into his new task. He restored order in Gaul, drove out the barbarians and imposed his

[1] Julian, *Ep.* 58. [2] *Letter to the Athenians.* [3] *Ep.* 55.

authority upon some of the tribes beyond the Rhine. These successes, and the way he shared in all the hardships of his troops, made the latter his devoted and enthusiastic supporters. Four years after his appointment his growing power and popularity appear to have alarmed Constantius, who ordered him to dispatch to the East a large part of his forces. There was sufficient danger from Persia to make this request appear reasonable, but it was in effect a threat to Julian's power and security. His army, passionately devoted to him, interpreted the order in that way. Those who had been ordered eastwards refused to march, and they mutinied in February 360, declaring Julian their emperor with the title of Augustus. Constantius refused to recognize this new position. Julian set out against him. But Constantius died suddenly in November 361 and Julian became sole Augustus and ruler of the entire Empire.[1]

Without renewing the ancient persecutions of Christianity he now gave full support to a revival of the old cults, and to general religious toleration. All men, whether pagan, Christian or Jew, were allowed to worship freely. Moreover he withdrew the support which the state had hitherto given to orthodox Christian belief, and all persecution of heretics ceased. Temples to the old gods were rebuilt and restored and their public worship was resumed.[2]

As heretic and orthodox Christian now struggled with one another on equal terms, old grievances were remembered and old debts of vengeance repaid. In Alexandria the bishop was lynched by his fellow Christians. Moreover violence broke out in several provinces between the adherents of Christ and the newly encouraged followers of the old gods. Two men, evidently Christians, were arrested in Gaza on a charge of attempting to destroy temples, and they were lynched by an angry mob. In Caesarea the Christians destroyed the Temple of Fortune. The government of Julian, in punishing the offenders, seemed always to bear down more lightly upon pagan than upon Christian criminals. Finally, Julian forbade any Christian to teach literature in the schools.[3]

For three years, until his death in battle against the Persians, Julian strove for a revival of the ancient ways. His edicts had full effect in

[1] A. H. M. Jones, *The Later Roman Empire*, chapter iv, note 16.
[2] Ibid., note 17.
[3] Ibid., note 20.

Britain, and we can imagine three years of strife and difficulty for the congregations of the island. Whether there were outbursts of violence, as there were elsewhere, we do not know. But we do know that Julian's policies were actively pursued in Britain, for at Cirencester there has been found a stone that bears an inscribed dedication 'to the old religion'. It was erected by no less a personage than L. Septimius, governor of one of the four British provinces during the reign of Julian. It thus shows that pagan cults were being as actively encouraged by the official authority in Britain as elsewhere. No doubt the same authority that raised the altar would have done all possible to discourage Christianity. From the schools of Britain Christian teachers of literature were withdrawn. From the churches of Britain the wealth was drained away. Throughout the island the faith suffered a setback. It was a setback without the drama of persecution or the telling witness of martyrs. It was rather a series of pinpricks, of tedious changes in taxation, of partiality by magistrates, and the public flaunting—so painful to Christian eyes—of reopened pagan temples and of new altars to the ancient gods who had seemed, during the golden age of Constantine and his immediate successors, to have been banished for ever.

But the setback was brief and the result ephemeral. We have seen from an earlier chapter that archaeological evidence of Christianity in Britain runs right through the fourth century.

Julian's brave attempt to defeat the Galilean (an attempt that did not have its origins in rancour, hatred or bitterness, but in a sincere love for the great days of the Hellenic world) had no permanent effect.

9

MAXIMUS

IT WAS towards the end of the fourth century that direct Roman power in Britain came to an end. For many years thereafter the Christian inhabitants of the island strove to continue Roman methods and Roman civilization, but effective contacts with Rome itself had largely ended. Roman armies no longer garrisoned the walled cities and the great forts along the coast. The Empire was crumbling throughout Europe, and the island of Britain (apart from a few isolated attempts by Rome) was now more and more left to her own resources.

The main preoccupation of the army in Britain during the years preceding its departure had been the defence of the island against the inroads of barbarians from the north and from Ireland, and of sea raiders from the Continent. More than once large areas had been overrun, and early in 360 Julian had sent an expeditionary force to drive out the Picts and Scots who were ravaging the frontier districts. A few years later, in 368, there were fresh attacks on the island. The Picts swept over Hadrian's Wall; the Scots in the west rose in simultaneous revolt; the Franks and Saxons, acting in concert, landed an army in the south-east. It seemed that the final chapter of the story of Roman Britain had ended and that the barbarians had finally taken control of the island.

One of Rome's greatest generals, Count Theodosius, was sent to restore the position and to drive out the barbarians. He was completely and dramatically successful. Order and peace returned and the orderly life of city and countryside continued as before.

Theodosius resumed his continental command, but some of his officers remained in Britain. Among these was a Spaniard, Magnus Maximus. He was an able and experienced officer who had evidently won the admiration and loyalty of the legions in Britain. For some years later, in 383, they proclaimed him as their emperor.

Confident of his ability, driven by ambition and goaded by envy of the imperial state of his former comrade-in-arms, the younger

Theodosius, who was now Emperor of the East, Maximus accepted the title bestowed upon him by the legions. To hold this title in Britain was not enough. He embarked all the best troops of the island and sailed with them to the Continent, to wrest the reality of power from Gratian, Emperor of the West. His armies from Britain were successful and Gratian committed suicide. Maximus entered Rome, and the title that he had received in the northern land of Britain he now bore proudly in the Eternal City itself.

Like Constantine, his great exemplar, Maximus was a Christian. His coins bear the Chi-Rho monogram, and the Christian community in Britain rejoiced that the island had again created an emperor. For five years Maximus ruled in the west, keeping the army of Britain with him, until his death in battle against Theodosius (388). So ended his dream of imperial greatness, and so ended effective Roman rule in Britain. For the armies of Maximus never returned. Thenceforward the forts of Hadrian's Wall were never garrisoned, and no Roman troops were ever again stationed permanently in Britain.

From this time forward Britain was no longer part of the Empire. She was to create local emperors, obscure and ineffective men, whose appointment symbolized the anxiety and eagerness of the Britons to continue the ancient forms of government and to remain, even nominally, a part of the Roman world. In fact, however, the departure of the legions under Maximus spelled the end of Roman rule.

Britain continued for many generations more as a Christian country, and as a country in which Roman forms of government and Roman designations of office persisted. But, effectively, she was now alone, growing as remote and separate from the continent of Europe as she had been before the coming of the armies of Claudius three hundred and fifty years before.

10

A CHRISTIAN GOVERNOR

ALTHOUGH effective Roman rule in Britain had ended with the adventure of Maximus, some contact and communication continued. Moreover attempts were still to be made by Rome to retrieve the lost island, to rebuild its shattered defences and to bring it once more into the community of the Empire. It is at this time of disaster and defeat, and of Rome's last organized efforts to save the diocese of Britain, that individual Christians begin to emerge from the shadows that now increasingly obscure events.

The Emperor Theodosius, whose early years as a young officer had been spent in Britain, took such steps as seemed possible to save the island from final and overwhelming ruin. In 394 he appointed a new *Vicarius*, or Governor-General of Britain. Clearly the new appointment was one of great importance. The garrisons gone, the island suffering continued raids and attacks at the hands of the Picts from the north and of the Scots from Ireland, the office of *Vicarius* of Britain required a man of outstanding ability. It might have been expected that the new governor would be a man of outstanding administrative skill and stout-hearted resolution, in whose qualities the Emperor had full faith. His name was Chrysanthus, son of Marcianus, and we know that he was a Christian, for he was later appointed Bishop of the Novatian Church in Constantinople.[1]

It was during the civil governorship of Chrysanthus that Theodosius sent Stilicho, Master of the Armies of the West and the Empire's greatest general, to reorganize the broken defences of Britain (395–9). It is clear that Theodosius saw the task of defending the island as one of imperial importance, for he would not otherwise have spared Stilicho, whose military skill was the shield of Europe against the growing thrusts of the barbarians. In the greatness of Stilicho we have a measure of the greatness of Chrysanthus, a man thought worthy to be the civil colleague of Rome's most distinguished commander at a time

[1] *Socrates*, vii. 11.

of immense difficulty, when Britain lay under the louring clouds of imminent and thunderous peril.

Moreover his appointment and his subsequent career give us a vivid glimpse, however brief, of Britain at that time. Now with a Christian governor at her head—a man for whom Christianity was not merely a formal faith but who was to find fulfilment of his career within the Church and as a churchman—she was suffering raid and invasion bravely and not without hope. Communications with the Empire were still open. At the end of his term of office in the northernmost province of the Empire, lying far in the western seas, Chrysanthus could travel (the barbarians notwithstanding) across the width of Europe, and take up a bishopric in the city of Constantinople.

In spite of barbarian invasions the long roads of Europe were still open, and the seas could still be traversed. Travellers could still journey from Britain to the eastern capital of the dying Empire and the Christian community of Europe was still a unified whole. Chrysanthus, once governor of Britain, could become a bishop in Constantinople and make the long journey to his new see.

His career not only reminds us of the regular exchange of men and ideas between Britain and the eastern provinces; it also shows that a career in the Church was not incompatible with an earlier career in the service of the state. Later we shall meet another bishop who, like Chrysanthus, had held secular office, and who was able to bring Britain not only spiritual comfort but administrative and indeed military skill.

4

THE FIFTH CENTURY

1

SLAVE AND PRIEST

THE closing years of the fourth century were years of trouble for Britain. The army, as we have seen, had sailed to the Continent under Maximus. Victory, tiptoe in expectation and crowned with imperial laurel, had beckoned them. But she had stayed with them only briefly. Defeat and exile had been their final fate, and the island of Britain, all defences broken, lay open to the raids of rovers and pirates from the wild lands across the seas.

It was one such raid from the shores of Ireland that proved to be the beginning of a long career of devoted work and high adventure for a young British Christian. He became the first of many Britons who then and later were to carry the Christian religion into many lands across the seas.

At the time of Maximus's campaign on the Continent there was living at a place called in the manuscripts *Bannavem Tabernae* (probably somewhere near the Bristol Channel, perhaps in Glamorganshire) a well-to-do Christian named Calpurnius. He was a deacon of the Christian Church and also a minor official known as a decurion. This office was originally one of the junior magistracies in Rome, but had become a local and municipal post in the provinces. Calpurnius would have had a seat in the assembly that governed the district where he lived, and can be thought of as the equivalent of a modern town councillor.

Calpurnius's father also was a Christian. His name was Potitus and he was a priest. Since Calpurnius must have been born in the 350's or 360's, Potitus provides interesting evidence that not all priests were celibate in the early Church in Britain; there is other evidence to the same effect in respect of the Church in Gaul at the same time.[1]

Probably some time after 372 Calpurnius's wife gave birth to a boy.

[1] The earliest enactment of celibacy in the Western Church is the 33rd canon of the Synod of Elvira (*c.* 306).

His parents called him Succat, which is clearly of non-Roman origin, and corresponds to the modern Welsh *hygad*, warlike. This suggests that in spite of the Romanized names of both father and grandfather the family was native British and not Roman immigrant. The Romanized names of Potitus and Calpurnius further suggest that Christianity was now closely identified with the Roman power and that, on baptism, Roman names were frequently adopted. Indeed this seems to have happened in the case of young Succat himself. For when he was baptized he was given the new and Romanized name Magonus or Imigonus.[1]

Succat was brought up as a Christian and received a good education. The Christian faith of his youth made a deep and lasting impression upon him and endured steadfastly through the many adventures and hardships he was to suffer. As a boy no doubt he enjoyed a settled and peaceful life. His father, a man of some wealth and considerable official standing, would have seen to it that the boy had a secure and happy childhood. He would have grown familiar with the stories of the early days of Christianity in Britain, and of the martyrs, priests and teachers who had dwelt there. Surrounded by the comforts and treasures that had no doubt been accumulated by his family over three generations, with access to books that his grandfather had possessed, Succat led a life of warmth and comfort.

Then, just as he had put boyhood behind him, when he was sixteen years old, tragedy came to the comfortable villa of Calpurnius. A gang of raiders from Ireland, secure in the knowledge that effectively there were no more troops in Britain, sailed across the dividing sea, hauled their ships up some sheltered beach and marched inland in search of loot and slaves. They broke into Calpurnius's villa, overcoming such resistance as the family and servants could offer, ransacked the stately rooms, seizing as plunder whatever they could of coin and of such objects of gold and silver as may have adorned the house of the prosperous decurion. In the hubbub of the raid and the hurly-burly of the fight they also seized young Succat, their hearts eager with anticipation of the profit to be made by selling such a young man as a slave once they were safely back in their native Ireland. In spite of the bitterness of the

[1] It should be remembered that the surviving accounts of St Patrick are obscure and not seldom contradictory. The present narrative is one of several possible reconstructions of his life.

struggle, neither Calpurnius nor his wife were slain, for we know that the boy was to revisit them after many years. Nor, it seems, was the house burned or destroyed. The raid was as brief as it was sudden, and Calpurnius was left in his ravaged home, to mourn the loss of his dear son and to be filled with nightmare thoughts of the boy's likely and unspeakable fate.

We do not know for sure when this happened. The sources are late and the tales confused. But we know that Succat was sixteen, and we know that he was sold as a slave to a king who began to reign in 388. Thus he must have been born not more than sixteen years before, that is in 372 at the earliest. But if he had been born (as is possible) a few years later, in 389, he would have been sixteen in 405, at a time when the Irish are known to have been raiding Britain.

Succat was hustled away by his triumphant captors, who led him down to the sea and to their waiting ships. Across the tossing waves of the sea they sailed, far out of sight of any land, on what for Succat must have been a strange and terrible voyage. They sailed into the setting sun, and made landfall on the eastern shores of Ireland. There the plunder was divided; there too young Succat was sold as a slave.

His owner was King Milchu of the kingdom of Dalaradis, which probably lay in County Antrim in north-eastern Ireland. No doubt the men who had sold him told with exaggeration of the fine villa where they had taken him, and of his wealthy and patrician background. Perhaps young Succat's own bearing and manner supported their claim and added to its likelihood. King Milchu, his owner, gave him a new name which he was to bear throughout his years of slavery and—with a difference—for the rest of his life. The king called him Cothrige—a name given apparently in irony and contempt. For in the old Irish tongue the sounds 'c' and 'p' were interchangeable, and Cothrige is Pothrige, from the Latin *Patricius*, the Noble One.

To add to his sense of triumph in owning as a slave an aristocrat from the Roman province, the king made the boy his swineherd. For many years Succat, now Cothrige the slave, tended the king's pigs in the hills and valleys of his barbarian kingdom. There is a tradition that he lived near the valley of Broughshane, and there, far from his parents and from any Christian friends, he grew to lonely manhood, with the long lean pigs of Dalaradis as his chief companions. But all the while. through the indignities and hardships of his task, through the sarcasm and contempt of the king and the king's household, Cothrige the slave remembered his faith and planned his escape.

For seven weary years he served his master. Then, at the age of twenty-three, he stole from the king's farm, made his way to the coast and found a ship whose master was buying Irish wolf-hounds, already famous, for shipment to the Continent. The captain was sympathetic to the young runaway and gave him passage to Gaul. This must have been between 395 at the earliest (since King Milchu began to reign in 388 and Cothrige became his slave at sixteen) and 412.

Once in Gaul he was in Christendom again, among people who spoke Latin—the language of his own boyhood. About two months after his arrival he made his way to the great monastery of Lerins. It is probably from there that he revisited Britain, and saw once again the half-remembered land of his boyhood and his father's house, where he found his parents, still living in the old home that had been the scene of his capture. This story furnishes evidence that life in Britain was still being carried on normally, raids and piracy notwithstanding. Communications with the Continent were still open; families, after the slaughter and pillage of a barbarian raid, with sons or daughters sold into slavery, picked up the pieces of their broken world and life somehow continued.

It was probably during this brief sojourn in Britain that he had his famous dream. A man came to him carrying a number of letters, and the first words in the one that he took were 'The voice of the Irish'. Then he heard the voices of men whom he had known during his captivity, begging him to visit them again and to walk among them.

Straightaway, therefore, he returned to Gaul, this time to Auxerre, in order to prepare for his mission. In due course he was ordained by Bishop Amator, taking the name he had received in slavery, but changing it back from the Irish Cothrige to its original Latin form Patricius. By this name he was known for the rest of his long life, and by it he is known today throughout the world: St Patrick, Apostle of Ireland. In 418 Amator was succeeded as Bishop of Auxerre by St Germanus, with whom Patrick seems to have remained for another fourteen years. During that time the holy prelate would have listened with interest to Patrick's stories of his boyhood in Britain, whose contacts with Gaul were less frequent and close than they once had been. He would have learned also something of the little-known island of Hibernia, which the arm of Rome had never reached. Moreover in the early years of the fifth century heresy had begun to spread among the Christian communities of Ireland, to such an extent that Pope Celestine I appointed Palladius, a deacon, to go there and teach the true doctrine. Palladius, however, did not succeed in his task. A substitute had to be found, and Germanus consecrated Patrick for the Irish mission.

So Patrick, putting aside the comforts and prosperity of life in civilized Gaul, took ship with a few companions to the wild and hostile country that had once enslaved him and that had caught his imagination. The year was 432, thirty years after his flight from bondage. He was now in late middle age, a time at which not many men seek a new life and new adventures.

According to the stories, he landed at the mouth of the River Vartry in Wicklow and was accorded a most hostile reception. The local people hurled a shower of stones at him and his companions, one of whom had his front teeth knocked out.

Undeterred by this unpromising start, Patrick and his companions, one at least mopping the blood from bruised lips and torn gums, sailed northward and landed on a small island, which became known in the seventh century as *Insula Patricii*, the Isle of Patrick, and which is named Innespatrick to this day.

Continuing his journey by ship, Patrick sailed across Strangford Lough to the mouth of the River Slaney and made his first convert, Dichu, a local chief. The latter gave him a barn for use as a church. The Celtic word for a barn is *sabhal* and the church there, known as the Church of Saul, has remained to this day a centre of Christian worship.

Patrick then led his party towards the territory of King Milchu, his former master. Fearful that his one-time slave had come to demand an awful vengeance for the long years of captivity and indignity, the king consulted his Druids. They prophesied that Patrick the slave would triumph over Milchu the king. The solemn prophecies of Druids were not to be disregarded. The king in despair set fire to all his household goods and perished in the flames.

Next Patrick deliberately challenged the authority of Laoghaire, High King of Ireland. At Easter time he entered the dominions of the High King, who was presiding over a gathering of all the chiefs of

Ireland on Tara. Laoghaire, in accordance with ancient royal custom, had ordered that on this occasion no fires should be lit in his dominions until he himself had kindled his own fire on Tara as a sign of his authority. Patrick challenged the king by lighting his own Easter fires on the Hill of Slane, a defiant act symbolic of his confidence that the power of his religion was greater than the power of temporal kings.

King Laoghaire saw the challenge of Patrick's fires from Tara and marched on Slane to avenge this insult to his authority.

Then, say the stories, Patrick tried to convince his adversaries of the truth of his faith. The disputations between King Laoghaire and his Druids on the one hand, and Patrick on the other, are overlaid with legend, and ornamented with improbable marvels. But from them Patrick emerged triumphant, having convinced the king and his court of the truth of the new religion. Great numbers of the Irish were baptized, including King Laoghaire himself.

For many years Patrick travelled the separate kingdoms of Ireland, making converts and founding churches. When he died—some say at the improbable age of 120—Christianity was firmly planted in Ireland and centres of worship set up throughout the land.

Patrick died near the Church of Saul, the spot where he had dedicated his first church in the barn of Dichu, his labours completed and his dream fulfilled.

2

NORTH OF THE WALL

THE frontiers of Roman Britain were for the most part the wide waters of the sea. But there was one land frontier, for the whole of the island had never been conquered. Northwards were the untamed and independent tribes of Caledonia, made secure by their valour and by the wild mountains where they dwelt. From the civilized lands of the Roman province they were divided by the great Wall, built in the time of Hadrian, stretching from the eastern to the western sea. This Wall was one of the most dramatic landmarks of the ancient world. Southwards lay the Roman province, linked by roads, ports and ships to all the lands of the Empire and, across them, to the marbled glories of Rome itself. Northwards dwelt the barbarians, the tattooed tribes whom the Romans called Picts—the painted men. And beyond the country of the Picts lay the remote northern ocean, leading to far and unknown lands of ice and strange screaming birds.

The Wall was now deserted; its garrisons had sailed with Maximus. The guard-rooms and signal towers were empty; the neglected doors swung in the northern winds, and the grass grew long on the deserted parade grounds of the vanished legions.

Now, when Rome's military power was gone from the island, her new power of religion was to cross the Wall into the wild lands, and was to make settlements beyond the limits set by the army.

Before Maximus had squandered the army of Britain, to buy himself a brief and doomed period of sovereignty, a boy had been born into one of the noble Christian families of Britain. That boy was named Ninian, and according to one story his father was a king in Britain.[1] From the later events of his life, for which dates are available, we know that he must have been born round about the year 350. His father caused him to be baptized and he was given a good education. Then, some time during the pontificate of Pope Damasus (366–84), he went to Rome and stayed there for many years. He was ordained a priest, and later consecrated bishop by Pope Siricius in 394. Not long afterwards he was sent by the Pope to evangelize western Britain.[2]

His journey back to his homeland took him into Gaul. There, according to his biographer,[3] he stopped to visit Martin, one of the most eminent churchmen of the period. Martin was subsequently canonized and is known to history as St Martin of Tours. He was a leading figure in the Gallic Church, with which the Church in Britain had close contact and frequent communication. It was natural therefore that Ninian should visit him on the way to his new post.

Martin had a monastery which was known as *Loco Tegiacum* or *Loco Teiac*. The name is of Celtic origin, and in the old Celtic tongue the word for white or gleaming is *Leug* or *Leuq*. The word for house is

[1] Ailred, *De Vit. Nin.* [2] Ibid. [3] Ibid.

Tigos. (A shanty is a *shan-tig*, an old house.) The additional letters *ac* are a diminutive. Thus *Loco Tegiac(um)* may well be *Leug Tigiac*, or 'Little White House'.[1] Ninian spent some time with Martin and no doubt visited and worshipped in the White House Monastery. Although the languages of Gaul and of Britain were different both tongues were Celtic. So the Gaulish name of the monastery would have been meaningful and evocative to Ninian the Briton. Later events show that Martin made a profound impression upon Ninian. His days in the monastery were memorable, and indeed it is not impossible that he there underwent some deep spiritual experience. Perhaps it was in that place, under the guidance of the wise and holy Martin, that Ninian formed the idea of teaching the message of Christianity to the barbarians north of the Wall, and of converting the fierce and mysterious tribes in the tall hills of mist and heather. He would go beyond the deserted defences of the Wall, to the wild country where there were no Roman arms to shield him and no Roman law to protect him. He would take the news of Christ to the tattooed barbarians, the Picts, who had for so long been the envious and greedy enemies of the Roman province.

So Ninian left the monastery of Martin and travelled northwards to the Channel. Some say that Martin sent trained builders and stonemasons to bear him company,[2] so that churches might be built in the places where he preached. Ninian with his companions crossed the narrow sea from Gaul and set foot again in his native Britain, some twenty-five or thirty years after he had left it to travel to Rome. Much had changed and many things had deteriorated since his departure. London had been renamed Augusta. The old garrisons had departed and at least one German tribe, the Alemanni, had been settled in Britain to stiffen the defences. The Picts had swept over the frontier, had crossed the Wall and had marched south, burning and pillaging. Pitched battles had been fought in the once peaceful province, as a Roman expeditionary force under the command of Stilicho, the outstanding general of Europe, strove to restore order and peace again.

Undeterred by the growing danger, Ninian travelled northwards, crossed the Wall and entered the hostile territory of the independent

[1] A. B. Scott, *The Rise and Relations of the Church of Scotland.*
[2] Scott, op. cit.

tribes to bring the message of Christ to the barbarians. He entered what is now Galloway and there began his mission.

There is some slight evidence that, although lying outside the frontiers of the Roman province, Galloway was ruled by a prince or chieftain friendly to the Roman power and appointed by them, for one of the Welsh royal genealogies tells us that Galloway's princely house traced its descent from 'Maxim Wledig'. Now this is the name in Welsh legend of Maximus, the British commander, who had taken the armies of the province to the Continent in 383. The Welsh tale cannot be taken literally, and we are not entitled to believe that it was a son of Maximus who was sent to govern Galloway. But the story may well embody a true tradition that a governor of the area had been appointed by Maximus and had ruled with his authority. Later, when Maximus had gone, and with him had departed the full power of Roman rule, this governor may well have set himself up as a king and so have founded a dynasty. For Roman Britain broke up into many kingdoms when Roman rule perished, and the ruler of Galloway may well have become king of his broad lands.

The Welsh genealogy gives the name of the first ruler as 'Annwn', which is a distortion of the Roman name Antonius. As we shall see, Ninian was in Galloway within fourteen years of Maximus's departure. So Antonius might have been still the ruler, either as governor or as king. We may be sure that Ninian would have visited Antonius (or possibly his son) and that, as Roman citizen to Roman citizen, would have sought and obtained his permission to settle in Galloway and to teach the Gospel to the people.

Certainly his mission was more successful than might have been possible had he been thrusting into completely tribal country without the friendship of a sympathetic ruler, for he is said to have converted all the Picts south of the Grampians. Bede [1] tells us that all the Picts in the south 'who dwell this side of the mountains' left the errors of idolatry, having been converted by Ninian's preaching. Again we see the support of the local ruler, without which Ninian could never have travelled so far through a strange land of which the inhabitants had for so long been hostile to Roman rule and to all that Rome stood for.

We know the names of the tribes in Galloway, for Ptolemy the Geographer, who wrote some two hundred and fifty years earlier, tells

[1] *Hist. Ecc.* iv.

us that this part of Scotland was inhabited by the Novantae and the Selgovae. We know that the latter survived in the area for many years, for the town of Selkirk takes its name from them. There is no reason to suppose that the Novantae were any less enduring.

A picture of Ninian's activities begins to emerge. We see him coming to the land of Antonius, which was inhabited by the Pictish tribe of the Novantae. Although traditionally enemies of Rome, they had accepted Antonius as their governor and later as their king. Antonius himself may well have been a Christian. Certainly he was favourably inclined to the bishop, who was thus enabled to travel as far north as the heathered highlands, converting the hitherto pagan and idolatrous tribes to the new faith.

Later he was permitted to build a church for his converts among the Picts. This too suggests support of the local ruler, for the church was no hastily erected building of timber or of wattle and daub. Bede tells us that it was built of stone, unlike the usual structures of the local people. Here again we glimpse the figure of Antonius or his successor, for this was no mere grant of land: the work of many men must have gone into the building, stone had to be quarried and transported, food for the masons and labourers had to be provided, and wide resources placed at the disposal of Ninian. Perhaps Antonius ought to be remembered as the patron and joint founder of Christianity in the lands north of the Wall.

Antonius's grandson was called Tudwal, and there is a poem written in Galloway about 800, when the Romans had been gone three hundred years and more, which celebrates the legend of Ninian and tells us of his meeting with Tudwal. The dates make it unlikely that this tale is true, but here again is evidence of a tradition, however shadowy, that Ninian met and worked with the local kings of the region.

Bede records that Ninian's church was dedicated to St Martin. This means that it must have been consecrated after 397, the year of Martin's death.[1] Ailred, the twelfth-century biographer of Ninian, tells us that news of Martin's death reached Ninian while the church was still being built. If this tale is true it gives us the exact date of the building.

Ailred was convinced that there was a close connection between

[1] *Hist. Ecc.* iv.

Ninian and Martin, for we must remember his statement that Martin sent stonemasons with Ninian to help in the building. Certainly Ninian must have brought with him, or sent for, men trained in the mysteries of stoneworking, for there would have been none locally. Moreover Ailred's words cannot be lightly disregarded merely because he was writing some seven hundred years after the events he describes. He referred to older material and tells us that he made use of the works of Bede. Further, he claims to have had access to 'a book on Ninian's life and miracles written by a barbarian'. The phrase suggests that the book was written in Galloway and that Ailred may have been able to make use of local written material which is now lost. His statements about the connection between Ninian and Martin, if derived from these sources, may well be true.

This link with St Martin is supported not only by the dedication of the church. The name given to the building reinforces the story, for Bede tells us that Ninian's church was commonly known as *Candida Casa*, or the White House. Bede explains this by saying that the house was built of stone. But the name is an exact Latin translation of the Celtic name of St Martin's monastery, *Loco Teiac*, the Little White House. This seems to give substance to the words of Ailred and to argue for the truth of his statements about the close link between the British missionary and the Gaulish churchman. Here, in a far land and among a recently pagan people, Ninian built his church and named it after the monastery of Martin where, in the old and settled land of Gaul, he had spent quiet days of prayer and discussion on his journey from Rome back to Britain.

Little now remains of the first church of Ninian. Later buildings stand on the spot; but the place still bears the name of Whithorn, echoing the earlier name *Candida Casa*, the first recorded centre of Christianity in Scotland. And to the east of the medieval church that now occupies the site archaeologists have found pieces of masonry that may be part of the walls of Ninian's building. These walls are constructed of local stone set in clay. The outside has been covered with a cream-coloured plaster, pieces of which were still adhering to the rough stone face of the wall. So *Candida Casa*, the White House, was once white indeed, its stout walls bright with their gleaming coat of plaster.[1]

[1] Radford and Donaldson, *Whithorn and Kirkmadrine*.

Though the church itself has vanished, several carved and inscribed stones remain that are witness to the great age of Christian worship in this area. They also furnish evidence that Christianity survived the death of Ninian himself and flourished through the succeeding centuries.

Oldest of these is a roughly squared stone pillar discovered in 1891, probably near to the site of the original church. It is inscribed:

(ET) DOMINV(M)
LAVDAMVS
LATINVS
ANNORV(M)
XXXV ET
FILIA SVA
ANN(ORVM) IV
(H)IC SI(G)NVM
FECERVT
NEPVS
BARROVA
DI

This is a memorial stone to a man named Latinus and the inscription, in translation, runs:

> *We praise the Lord! Latinus aged thirty-five, and his daughter aged four. This monument was erected here by his grandson Barrovadus.*

The style of the inscription shows this stone to date from the middle of the fifth century, a mere fifty years after the coming of Ninian.[1] Latinus, as a child, might well have known the missionary and could have been baptized by him.

Next in age is a stone pillar that used to stand by the roadside south of Whithorn. Upon it is carved a very early version of the sacred Chi-Rho monogram. The letter chi is made up of intersecting arcs of circles. On the right-hand side of the central feature there is the letter rho, now latinized to R. The whole lies within two concentric circles and beneath it is carved a shaft. The style is similar to examples from the eastern parts of the Empire, and the carving may well date to

[1] Radford and Donaldson, op. cit.

the fifth century. Here again we may be in the presence of a stone associated with the original building. At some time after the stone was first inscribed, someone added the words:

(L)OCI
PETRI APV
STOLI

which means: *The place of Peter the Apostle.* This indicates that the stone was used to mark a site where there was some feature, a cemetery or an oratory, sacred to St Peter. Oratories were not uncommon in Celtic monasteries, and they frequently contained a relic of the saint to whom they were dedicated. The lettering on the stone was probably done during the seventh century. It has been suggested that it may have replaced an earlier stone that marked the place where there was kept a relic brought by Ninian himself. What the inscription certainly shows is that Christian worship continued with no break during the sixth and seventh centuries.

West of Whithorn is the ancient site of Kirkmadrine. Two stones, that were until recently used as gateposts at the entrance of the old burial ground, again take us back to the fifth century and so possibly to the days of Ninian himself. Upon each is carved the Chi-Rho monogram in a simple and early form. The letter chi is a simple upright cross; the vertical stroke, by the addition of a small loop, serves as the letter rho in its original Greek form. The whole is set within a circle.

On one stone, above the circle, is carved:

A ET O

This is the Latin version of the Greek letters alpha and omega, used as a symbol of Christ (*I am Alpha and Omega, the beginning and the end* [1]). Below, in good Latin and well-cut letters, is the inscription:

HI(C) IACENT
S(AN)C(T)I ET PRAE
CIPVI SACER
DOTES IDES
VIVENTIVS
ET MAVORIVS

---

[1] Rev. xxi. 6.

This means *Here lie the holy and leading priests Ides, Viventius and Mavorius*. The form of the Chi-Rho monogram and the style of the lettering date the stone to the fifth century.[1] The names of the three priests, upon whose grave this stone once stood, are interesting, for Mavorius is a Celtic name, and these three men may have been among the first converts and followers of Ninian.

On the second stone the Chi-Rho monogram is similar, but the letters A and O do not appear. It too bears an inscription, recording the name Florentius and another now indecipherable. Like its fellow, it was once a gravestone and, again, Florentius may have been a contemporary of Ninian.

Also from Kirkmadrine comes a similar stone with a cross carved in later style. Below it is the inscription:

INITIVM
ET FINIS

This means *the beginning and the end* and, like the letters A and O, is a reference to the Book of Revelations. This stone dates from about A.D. 600 and is further evidence of the continuity of worship in this region.[2]

Ninian lived out his life at Whithorn. Bede tells us that his body was buried in the church that he built. His grave is now lost, and the stones of his building are scattered. We see his work but faintly, and can catch only shadowy glimpses of his life. We see him working with the support of the local ruler. Fleetingly, and with no certainty, we see the names of those who may have been his priests or members of his flock. But the little we know is enough to tell us that by the late fourth century, two hundred years before Augustine, a Christian Briton had ventured into the wild lands north of the Wall, and had there carried the message of Christ to the enemies of Rome.

[1] Radford and Donaldson, op. cit. [2] Ibid.

Coin of the Emperor Constantine the Great

Coin portrait of Helena, Constantine's Christian mother, who according to legend was a Briton

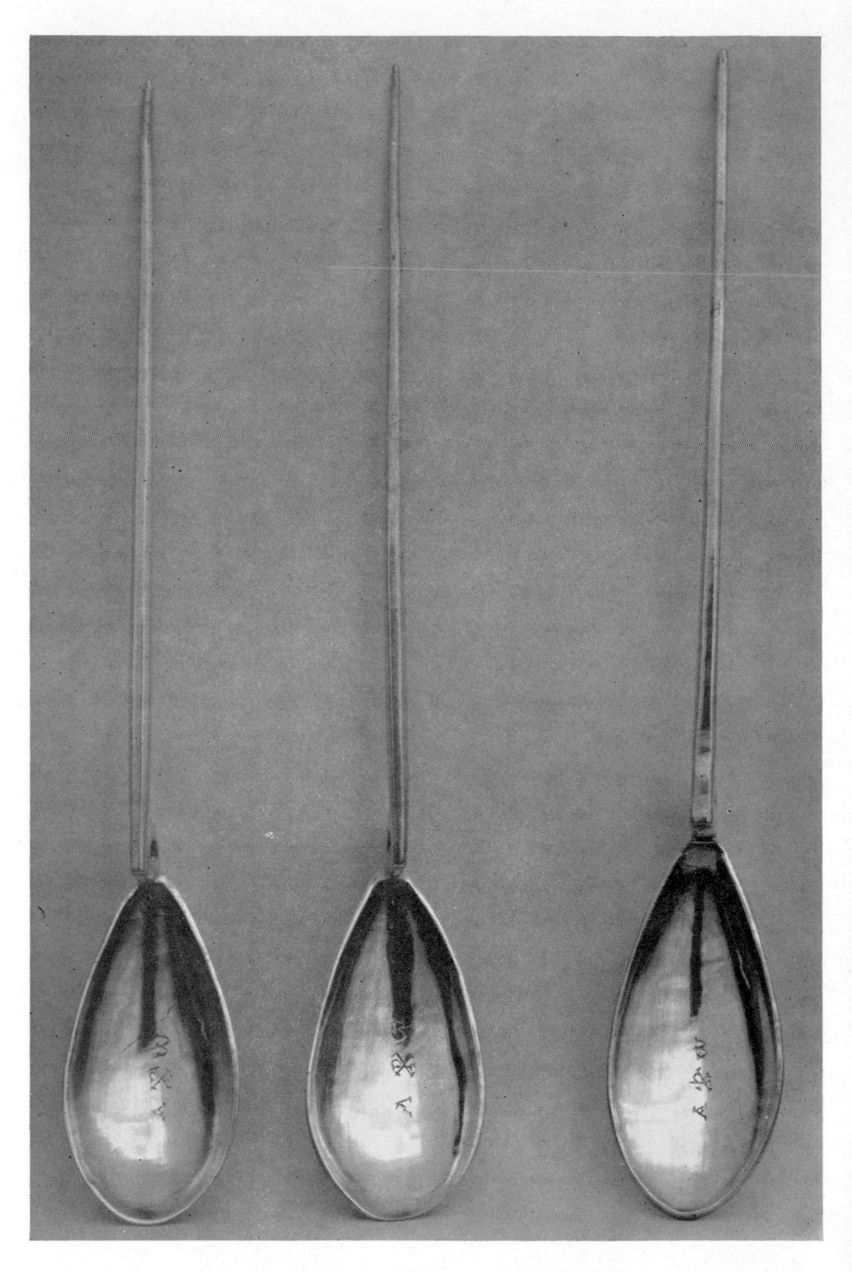

Silver spoons bearing the Chi-Rho monogram, from the Mildenhall Treasure

3

A BRITISH HERETIC

ABOUT thirty years before St Patrick left Auxerre for Ireland another Briton was developing a theological system that would arouse fierce controversy throughout the Christian world.

The origins of Pelagius (*c.* 360–*c.* 420) are obscure, to say the least. His name has been represented as a Greek form of the Celtic *Morgan*, 'sea-born'. Some say he was a layman, 'who must have come from the most Romanized social stratum in the most Romanized part of the country'.[1] Others hold him to have been a monk [2] from some monastery in Scotland or Ireland—a distant forbear, so to speak, of Columba, Columbanus and Adamnan.

At all events, Pelagius left his native land never to return, probably at the end of the fourth or the very beginning of the fifth century, and went to Rome. His purpose at that time, some say, was to study law. Whatever may have been his first intention his mind soon took a very different turn.[3] Morality was at a low ebb in the Eternal City in those days. Pelagius would have none of the age-old plea of 'human weakness'. His favourite motto was, 'If I ought, I can', and he set out to reveal the true powers of human nature. On one occasion he was listening to a friend reading aloud the *Confessions* of St Augustine, then recently published. When he heard the words, 'Give what Thou commandest, and command what Thou wilt', Pelagius, casting aside his normal composure, cried out: 'I cannot bear it!' What he could not bear was in fact the Augustinian doctrine of original sin and grace. He was doubtless unaware that the form of determinism preached by Augustine is to an orthodox Christian a *sine qua non* of sound ethical doctrine; he had convinced himself that Augustine's theory of man's

[1] R. G. Collingwood, *Roman Britain*, 1931.

[2] It is certain that he never received holy orders.

[3] His *Exposition of the Thirteen Epistles of St Paul* was written between 405 and 409.

total depravity, and the consequent bondage of his will, invalidated all human effort and saddled God with man's culpability.

Now Pelagius was of a gentle and retiring disposition, averse to the heat and clamour of debate. His beliefs, therefore, might not so quickly have attracted notice, had he not met and made a friend of one Coelestius, a lawyer turned ascetic and commonly supposed to have been an Irishman. Two more dissimilar personalities it would be hard to imagine. On the one hand the Briton, 'silent, smiling and reserved'; on the other that Irishman 'voluble, controversial, pugnacious'.[1] Coelestius took up the doctrines of Pelagius and cried them from the house tops, as Irishmen tend to do with matters dear to their hearts.

In 410 Rome was sacked by the Goths, and the two friends fled to Africa. There Pelagius once or twice met St Augustine, who was later to argue against his theories in no fewer than fifteen treatises. Pelagius, however, soon removed to Palestine, where he believed, not without some justification, that his opinions would encounter less hostility. Meanwhile Coelestius remained at Carthage, looking for ordination. But instead of the priesthood he received a summons from Bishop Aurelius, directing him to appear before a synod. There, by the mouth of Paulinus, a Milanese deacon, he was charged with six fundamental errors. He had taught, claimed Paulinus, first, that death would have been Adam's lot irrespective of his sin; second, that Adam's sin harmed no one but himself alone; third, that new-born infants enjoy the same state as did Adam before the Fall; fourth, that the whole human race does not die on account of Adam's sin, and will not owe its resurrection to the Resurrection of Christ; fifth, that the Law, no less than the Gospel, is a key to heaven; and, sixth, that even before the advent of Christ there lived men without sin.

Coelestius would not deny that such were his opinions, but he claimed them to be open questions never yet determined by the Church. Nevertheless he was condemned and excommunicated by the synod, made a fruitless appeal to Rome, and then sailed away to Ephesus, where he found a bishop who was willing to ordain him.

Meanwhile Pelagius had lived quietly in Palestine for several years, unmolested and revered by all. In the spring of 415 the formidable St Jerome was visited by an emissary of St Augustine, a Spanish priest named Orosius, who brought news of the proceedings at Carthage.

[1] Collingwood, op. cit.

Accordingly, in June, Pelagius was cited to appear before Bishop John of Jerusalem, charged with holding that a man may be without sin, provided he desires to be so. The case broke down, but in the following December Pelagius was confronted with a synod of fourteen bishops at Diospolis. This time he escaped condemnation by accepting the decrees of Carthage. He repudiated the doctrine of Coelestius, that the grace and help of God consist in free will and in the giving of the law and instruction; but he insisted that a man is able, if he so wills, to live without sin by virtue of the fact that God gives him this ability.

Despite his acquittal, the West was less indulgent. A second synod of Carthage, held in 415, condemned both Pelagius and Coelestius and wrote to Pope Innocent I, requesting his approval of the judgment. The Pope complied in a letter which is still extant. On the death of Innocent (417), Coelestius visited Rome, while Pelagius addressed a letter to the new pontiff, Zosimus. The Pope held a council, before which Coelestius argued to such effect that the fathers were satisfied that the doctrines of Pelagius had been misrepresented or misunderstood. In a third synod of Carthage, two hundred and fourteen bishops formally condemned the Pelagian doctrines in nine canons, which were sent to the Holy See with full explanations. Zosimus then reopened the case, cited and condemned the two culprits, published his *Epistola Tractoria* adopting the African canons and invited the bishops of Christendom to subscribe to it (418). Nineteen Italian prelates refused to do so and were deposed. Their leader, who may be regarded as the greatest theological advocate of Pelagianism, was the celebrated Julian of Aeclanum in Apulia.

In that same year Pelagius himself was banished from Rome by the Emperor Honorius, and we hear no more of him. Coelestius is known to have been at Constantinople ten years later, begging the assistance of Nestorius; then he too vanishes from history.

It must not be imagined that, because Pelagius was a Briton, his doctrines had originally much vogue in his homeland. The British Church as a whole extended to the canons of Carthage in 418 the same welcome that it had given to those of Nicaea in 325. The few Pelagians that found their way to Britain were refugees exiled from Rome by imperial decree in 421. Their presence here, as we shall see, was the cause of St Germanus's two missions to the island.

4

A CHRISTIAN WRITER

ABOUT the year 480, in what is today the city of Marseilles and which was even then a busy international port, a man named Gennadius wrote a book on the lives of famous men. Among the illustrious figures whose biographies he wrote there is one from Britain. His name was Fastidius, and Gennadius describes him as '*Britanniarum episcopus*', a Bishop in the British provinces.[1]

However, Gennadius tells us that Fastidius wrote a book which has survived and has come down to us across the dark chasm of the ages. The book, which was written in Britain between 420 and 430, is entitled *On the Christian Life*. It is addressed to Fatalis, a British lady.

This is the earliest surviving Christian work to have been written in Britain. Fastidius, who composed his work over a hundred and fifty years before the coming of St Augustine, is (with Pelagius) the pattern and precursor of all those men in the island who, in later ages, were to bring the art of writing into the service of religion.

He was a contemporary of Pelagius, but possibly a few years younger. His book shows him as a man of education and taste. It is written with grace and skill and in the past was wrongly ascribed to no less a divine than the great St Augustine of Hippo. Gennadius describes the book as expounding a doctrine that is worthy of God.

Fastidius addresses the lady Fatalis as '*dilectissima soror*'—'dearest sister'. The book is not profound, nor does it deal with points of subtle theology. It reflects the thoughts of a man living quietly and peacefully, possessed of firm and simple standards. Piety, gentleness and simplicity are the qualities that shine across the centuries. The picture it paints of Christianity in Britain is a pleasing one; it is a picture of a confident and sure faith, mature and safe-seeming, drawing on long tradition and settled beliefs.

There has been some argument as to whether Fastidius was a follower of Pelagius. R. G. Collingwood [2] states categorically that he

[1] Gennadius, *De Illustribus Viris*, 56. [2] *Roman Britain*, chapter xix.

was not, and this view is supported by the remark of Gennadius that the doctrine he expounded was 'worthy of God'. But Gennadius himself was influenced by Pelagius, as is clear from his book, so that his praise of Fastidius could be taken as evidence either way.

Moreover Fastidius appears, in at least two passages of his own work, to quote directly from Pelagius. True, he does not mention the latter by name. But when he writes of men who fall into sin through the *example* of Adam it seems fairly clear that we are hearing the voice of Pelagius. We know that followers of the British heretic were exiled from Rome in 421 and that some came to Britain and there began to preach their new doctrine. When Fastidius, at about this time, writes of men who sin by the example of Adam, it is impossible not to believe that, in his quiet and peaceful see, he had heard of the new teaching. Man had not inherited the sin of Adam, but had been corrupted merely by the example of his defiance of God's ordinance in the Garden of Eden. In another passage Fastidius describes how holy people should pray; his instructions echo precisely those of Pelagius.

Almost certainly, therefore, Fastidius had heard of the new teachings and had found them attractive. If so, he was not alone among the priests and laymen of Britain.

For by 428 the doctrines of Pelagius had gained so many followers in the island that the authorities of the Church sought help from the Continent, to combat the growing support for ideas that Rome and the East had alike declared to be heretical, and to have sprung from the darkness of error.

5

THE SOLDIER BISHOP

ALTHOUGH Pelagius never returned to Britain, living out his last unrecorded days in the eastern lands of the Empire, his ideas spread to the island of his birth. We have already seen how Fastidius, a gentle and kindly British bishop, echoed the writings of Pelagius in his own book on the Christian life. Whether Fastidius was a formal follower of Pelagius or not, he had clearly heard of and had been affected by these new ideas.

Britain at that time was an ideal refuge for fugitives from the Continent. The arm of the central government was now almost powerless in the four provinces. In 410 the Emperor Honorius had told the authorities in Britain that they must now look to their own defences. Direct Roman rule had ceased to exist. Thus men who were in conflict with the government or Church of Rome could settle safely in Britain, secure from interference or punishment. Yet to dwell in Britain was not to suffer exile from the comforts and companionship of the Roman world. The environment in Britain was still a Roman environment. The Church, the background of government, of Roman ideals and aspirations—all these remained.

So it was that in 421, when decrees were issued in Rome against the Pelagians, exiling them from the capital, some of them left the continent of Europe and crossed the Channel into Britain. There, secure from the interference of the Bishop of Rome and amid congenial and orderly surroundings, they began to teach their new beliefs to the people and to the priests.

One of these men was Agricola, son of a bishop named Severianus [1] who was also a Pelagian. But on reaching Britain neither he nor his companions were content to live quietly in the security of their new home. Passionately devoted to the ideas of Pelagius, which they saw as adding to the nobility and independence of mankind, the refugees travelled widely in Britain, preaching their new doctrine. They were

[1] Bede, *Hist. Ecc.* i. 17.

rapidly successful. As in Rome, when Pelagius and Coelestius began to teach, and as in the Churches of Africa, so now in Britain there were many who found the new thought attractive and stimulating. It may not be altogether fanciful to consider whether Pelagius, in developing his formal system of thought, was reflecting attitudes and beliefs that had existed in Britain during his youth. Perhaps he had made articulate the half-formed thoughts of many British Christians. Certainly his views, now that they were being formally preached, met with a sympathetic and swift response among the Britons. The heresy spread with dramatic speed, and dramatic was the step taken to combat it.

We are told that, as a result of Agricola's teaching, the new ideas had gravely polluted the beliefs of the Church in Britain.[1] This was no small and unimportant episode of arguments and discussions among Christians on points of interesting but insignificant aspects of doctrine. The leaders of the British Church saw it as a direct threat to the whole structure of Christian belief. If the grace of Christ was not necessary for salvation, then what function could the Church perform? If a man had not inherited the sin of Adam, but could by his own will live righteously and free from sin, then what was there left for priests to do? And if baptism, so long the special sign of Christian conversion and a central act in the theme of salvation, were no longer necessary for the washing away of original sin, what would happen to the whole structure of rites and ceremonics that bound Christians together and made the Church a unity?

It is significant that the orthodox bishops of Britain felt themselves to be quite inadequate to dispute the new teachings. The beliefs of Pelagianism were so plausible and so attractive that, although they were sure that the new doctrine was evil, they could find no convincing arguments to marshal against it. When it came to debate and disputation the followers of Pelagius were supreme. Frustrated, the bishops in Britain decided to seek help from their colleagues on the Continent.

The drastic nature of the steps they took, in appealing for help to the bishops of Gaul,[2] tells us how swiftly the heresy was spreading in

[1] Ibid.

[2] So Bede, i. 17. Other accounts suggest that the appeal was to Pope Celestine I, and that he first sent a deacon, Palladius (the same who later went to Ireland). Either there is confusion between the two missions, or the accounts can be reconciled by supposing that Palladius was sent by the Pope

Britain and how eloquent and persuasive were the exiles from Italy. For them to have been banished from Rome makes it clear that they were men who had taken a leading part in spreading Pelagianism there, and that they were considered both important and dangerous. The bishops in Britain were not ashamed to recognize their own inadequacies in arguing with men of this kind.

Schism and heresy were not the only dangers with which the island was now faced. There was also grave military peril. The year of their appeal was 428, and the Roman army had long since left the island. Britain had lost the shield which, for nearly four hundred years, had been held by the strong arm of Rome between her and her enemies. Across the grey North Sea and over the narrow waters of the Channel came the Saxon raiders from Germany. From the far north the Picts, now that Hadrian's Wall was no longer manned, raided southwards and marched insolently into the cities. The countryside lay at their mercy as the coastal towns and seaside villas lay at the mercy of the Saxon pirates.

So when the authorities in Britain asked for a man able and learned enough to dispute with and overcome the Pelagian heretics, they hoped also to receive material help against their pagan foes.

The man chosen was Germanus, Bishop of Auxerre. We have seen in the career of Chrysanthus how a man could hold a position in government and later be appointed bishop. Germanus too had held secular office before being appointed to the see of Auxerre. In his case the appointment had been a military one.

We are fortunate to have a very detailed account of his life, written by Constantius, a priest of Lyons.[1] Much that is legendary appears in this and other sources. Nevertheless we can see the basic facts through the shadows of legend. We know that Germanus came of a good family. His father and mother, Rusticus and Germanilla, were of noble descent. The boy, named after his mother, went to school at Lyons and received a good education. As a young man he went to Rome to study law.

On his return he married a girl called Eustachia and settled down to

---

with instructions to arrange with the bishops of Gaul for the appointment of someone to lead the undertaking. Celestine is regarded as the first pope to show a direct interest in the British Isles.

[1] *Gallia Christiana*.

an active military career. He was promoted to the rank of *Dux*, or general. As there were only six men of this rank in the whole of Gaul his military skill must have been outstanding. His duties seem, however, to have left him sufficient leisure to indulge his almost obsessional love of hunting. He seems to have been an early example of the active, outdoor, muscular Christian.

Not content with the mere pleasures of the chase, Germanus found a flamboyant way of celebrating and recording his triumphs. There was an old pear tree in which he hung, as trophies of his skill, the heads of the animals that had fallen to his bow and spear. As the days passed the strange fruit on the tree increased, and skull and horn mingled with the branches.

Amator, Bishop of Auxerre, saw the tree and its unusual harvest. Perhaps he thought that some ancient pagan tree-cult was being revived, and that the whitened bones were those of beasts sacrificed to old and evil gods. Whatever the cause, this obscenity was not to be tolerated. The good bishop remonstrated. But against Germanus, the headstrong soldier, mere remonstrances were vain. Finally, Bishop Amator had the tree felled and the trophies destroyed.

Germanus was furious. His reaction was fierce, simple and direct; he would kill the bishop, and he set out to do so.

Bishop Amator went to see Julian, the local Prefect. He asked, surprisingly, that Germanus should be made a priest, saying that there was no person fitter to follow him in the bishopric.

So Germanus was seized. Men forcibly cut his hair, and the headstrong soldier was ordained and nominated as Amator's successor. On Amator's death he was appointed to the bishopric and became a changed man. Devout, austere and learned, he was soon a leading figure in the Church, the wild days of his youth forgotten. Yet something of the soldier remained in the bishop, as he was to show.

This, then, was the man selected to visit Britain, to put down the heresy of Pelagius and perhaps to help the Britons in their growing wars. With him was sent Lupus, Bishop of Troyes, and in 429 the two men journeyed northwards to the coast of Gaul. There they took ship to cross the Channel. It must have been a daunting venture. No longer did the Roman warships guard the narrow seas, and at any time one of the terrible curved ships of the Saxon pirates might loom out of the grey mist.

But it was the elements and not the Saxons that proved the greatest hazard. At first the crossing was calm, and Germanus, worn out by his long journey across Gaul, had stretched himself out and was sleeping. When they were in mid Channel a storm blew up; the sky grew heavy with black clouds. The seas grew dark and the ship pitched and wallowed in the mounting waves. Germanus slept through the uproar. Even when a gust, stronger than the rest, tore away the sails Germanus did not stir.

Finally, when the exhausted sailors seemed to have lost all control of the vessel and when shipwreck seemed inevitable, Lupus and his companions wakened Germanus. He is said to have been more resolute than they (the courage of faith perhaps reinforced by the courage of an old campaigner), and he prayed aloud. He cast consecrated oil on the waves, in the name of the Trinity, and as if by a miracle the storm abated. The rest of the passage was calm and the wind favourable.

Their ship came safely into port. Waiting on the shore to greet them were large crowds.[1] Clearly the arrival of the two bishops was accounted a great event by the Britons, for contacts with other Roman provinces were now becoming rare. Hope and aid had so often come to the island from across the seas that the crowd must have joyfully taken the advent of the bishops as a sign that there would now be some mitigation of their difficulties and trials. Some of the more practical among the onlookers, less fearful of the spiritual perils of heresy than of the more visible danger of the wild Picts and raiding Saxons, may have muttered their regrets that it was a bishop who came and not a military commander to help them in their wars.

In fact Germanus was to be both the one and the other.

According to one story, he first turned to the task of correcting the heretical views of the folk in the towns and in the countryside. Every day he and his followers preached not only in the churches but in the streets and in the open fields. Many who had begun to follow the teachings of Pelagius were now reconverted to the orthodox faith. Germanus and his companion Lupus are said to have gained immensely in authority by their holiness, and their erudition and learning won them the obedience of all who heard them. The exiles from Italy, who had been led by Agricola and who had not met any among the British bishops able to defeat their arguments, were now confronted by two

[1] Bede, *Hist. Ecc.* i. 17.

adversaries as learned and as skilful as themselves. They began to withdraw from the public scene, and little was heard of them. But later they decided to challenge Germanus to public debate. Perhaps they realized that they must either give public proof of the rightness of their cause or suffer the humiliation of defeat by default.

Germanus accepted the challenge. Large crowds had gathered at Verulamium, the modern St Albans, to see this confrontation of the two beliefs. Men, with their wives and children, came to listen and to form their own judgments.

The Italians, who spoke first, bore themselves proudly. They spoke at considerable length and argued their case in detail, going carefully through the propositions of Pelagius. Germanus and Lupus followed and refuted all their arguments, quoting from the Scriptures to support the cause of orthodoxy, and to show that the teachings of the Church were based on the teachings of Holy Writ. As in the assemblies of bishops in the East, and as in the discussions in Rome, so here in Britain the attractive and plausible teachings of Pelagius's followers were defeated. But the triumph of Germanus was greater than that of the eastern bishops or of the Pope himself. For the exiles from Italy, who had remained unconvinced by the arguments in Rome and who had chosen exile rather than recantation, now admitted their error. The first and main purpose of the visit had been accomplished.

Germanus held a service of thanksgiving. After prayers had been said the tomb of St Alban, the martyr who had died about a hundred and twenty years earlier, was reverently opened. Within it Germanus laid certain relics which he had brought with him, so that the island of Britain might be hallowed by holy remains collected from many lands.

At this time Verulamium, like so many of the cities of Britain, was in a state of decay. The public buildings and monuments were growing shabby. Just outside the walls the once gorgeous theatre, with its proud columns and marble enrichments, had become a dump for the city's refuse. But the city was still a place of great importance to the Christians of Britain. The martyrdom of Alban was widely remembered and, shabby buildings and mean streets notwithstanding, it was a fitting place for the service of thanksgiving.

On leaving the sacred spot Germanus slipped and fell, injuring his leg. He was taken to a small house in a crowded area of the city where there was a cluster of thatched cottages. Fire broke out in one of them, leaping from thatched roof to thatched roof. Amid the smoke and turmoil crowds rushed to where Germanus was lying, anxious to move him to a safer place. But Germanus, with military calm, refused to panic and declined to leave. The fire passed over the house and he was unharmed. The event was taken as a miracle and added considerably to his reputation and authority.[1]

His spiritual work now completed, Germanus next turned to the military problems with which the island was beset.

For years now the Saxons had been raiding the coasts. To begin with, there had been merely swift and isolated acts of piracy. But now, safe in the knowledge that the legions had left, and that the people of Britain lacked officers, military skills and resolution, the Saxons were remaining for longer and longer periods in the province and were ranging deep into the inland areas. Moreover they had established contacts with the Picts north of the Wall and had made common cause with them against the Britons.

In the spring of 430 the news of this new danger reached the south. The Britons turned to Germanus for help and advice. Germanus and Lupus travelled swiftly to the point of danger, which was no doubt somewhere in the north of the province, where the Picts had joined their savage forces with those of the still more savage Saxons.

Germanus remembered his former career as a *Dux* in Gaul and set up his camp. But he also remembered his present duties as priest and bishop. Easter was approaching; at his camp he therefore ordered a timber church to be built within the defence works. There he baptized those of the Britons in the army who had not yet been entered as formal members of the Christian community. At the same time he studied the terrain with a soldier's eye, and planned his campaign.

The army at his disposal was very different from the trained troops of Gaul whom he had handled in days gone by, when he was still the headstrong and vigorous general who had quarrelled with Bishop Amator. The army of the Britons was badly trained and woefully short of arms. And he knew that the Picts and Saxons were aware of this and that they would not long delay their confident attack.

When the feast of Easter was over, Germanus the bishop became once again Germanus the commander. From the Britons in the camp he chose the most active and best trained, and he himself went out with

[1] Bede, *Hist. Ecc.* i. 19.

them among the hills and valleys to study the features of the surrounding countryside. In the path which the enemy must follow to reach his camp there lay a deep valley. Across one end of this there ran a river, and the hills that stood along the valley were steep and high. Here was an ideal place for an ambush, and here Germanus decided to give battle.

Now it was a matter of disciplining his own men, and of teaching them to obey orders, and to exercise that restraint which is the chief virtue of trained troops, and which distinguishes an army from an angry host.

When his scouts told him that the enemy was approaching the valley of his choice he led out his men, stationing them on the hills on either side. His orders were strict. Each man was to be hidden behind bush or boulder, making no sound. The Saxons and the Picts were to be allowed to cross the river at the head of the valley and to march forward unmolested. Germanus would give the signal for the action to begin when he knew that the right time had come. Until then no one was to move, nor was any sound to be made. And the signal would be the holy cry of 'Alleluia!' repeated three times. When this sign had been given the whole army was to echo the cry in order to strike terror into the hearts of the enemy, and was to move down the hillside in swift and unexpected attack.

The troops took up their positions, and the army lay silent under the blue spring sky, crouched in the scented grasses, lying in hollows and folds of the ground, shrinking behind grey rock and growing tree.

The murmur of the advancing host grew louder. The long column crossed the river and marched steadfastly and unknowing into the valley, confident, assured and unmindful of any trap. When the last of the barbarians were over the river Germanus rose, the standard held aloft in his hands. In a loud and commanding voice that echoed over the hills he called out his Christian battle-cry of 'Alleluia!' The whole army took up the shout and sprang from cover, leaping down the steep hills.

The enemy was shocked and bewildered as the quiet valley was suddenly ringed by armed and shouting men on the surrounding heights. Pict and Saxon alike thought of escape. They turned and fled, struggling with one another to be first to cross the river back to safety. Many drowned. Many others threw down their swords and shields and fled as swiftly as they could. The rout was complete and the victory total.[1]

[1] *Life of St Germanus*, xvii. 18.

The triumphant Britons, ill armed though they were, had scattered their foes and overcome their enemies decisively for the first time in many years.

Germanus returned to Gaul, but the renown of the Christian victory lived on. It took place less than a hundred and seventy years before the coming of Augustine. It became yet another strong memory of the Christians in the island and another potent reason why, when Augustine came, they felt his coming as an intrusion into a well-established Christian community, rich in faith, in tradition and in achievement.

6

A SAINT IN WALES

AMONG Patrick's fellow pupils under Germanus at Auxerre was a young man named Iltudus, known to us as St Illtyd. The details of his life have not reached us in trustworthy form.[1] Some have claimed, upon no satisfactory evidence, that he was a great-nephew of Germanus himself.

Illtyd appears to have been born in Armorica (modern Brittany), son of a nobleman called Biconys. Starting his career as what we might today describe as a senior civil servant, he later crossed to Britain and embraced the monastic life under St Cadoc in the great monastery at Llancarfan, a veritable nursery of saints, in Glamorgan.

Llancarfan was a power-house of prayer, but it was also a celebrated school. One of its later students was the historian Gildas, whom we shall presently meet again. The saint's own pupils may have numbered at least one future king, for Gildas, reproving a British chieftain, Maglocunus, tells him there is no excuse for his evil ways since he had been taught by one of the most cultured schoolmasters in the land.[2]

[1] The twelfth-century biography (printed in *Cambro-British Saints* from a MS. in the Cottonian Library) is a farrago of legend and a few basic facts.

[2] Gildas, *Ep.* xxxvi.

St Illtyd never returned to Gaul, but died *circa* 505 in the land of his adoption. He was buried in Brecknockshire and is one of the most famous of Welsh saints. His feast day appears to have been preceded by a solemn vigil, for there is a place in Brecknockshire that became known as Bedd Gwyl Illtyd—the Grave of St Illtyd's Eve—a name that seems to have some liturgical significance.

7

THE COMING OF THE PAGANS

DURING the campaign led by Germanus, the struggle of the Britons against the invading barbarians had, for the first time, been clearly identified with the Christian faith, and the Britons had now vividly seen their God as the Lord of Hosts and the God of Battles. Not only had their commander been a bishop of great and renowned holiness, many of the troops had been newly baptized in the little timber church within the camp and had gone into battle newly conscious of their Christian faith; the signal of their general, and the war-cry with which they had scattered their enemies, had been the Christian cry 'Alleluia!' The triumph which the army won in the ambushed valley gave an added strength and muscularity to the Christian faith throughout the island. Christianity now seemed to promise not only spiritual salvation, but immediate success on earth. A Christian army, scantily armed and with no warlike tradition to give strength to their hands or courage to their hearts, but with the help and blessing of their bishop-commander, had conquered the savage and determined host that had marched so confidently against them.

Even to face a Saxon army required more than ordinary courage. The reputation of the Saxons for ferocity and cruelty stood high throughout western Europe. Some forty years later Sidonius Apollinaris, Bishop of Clermont, wrote a letter to Namatius, a friend of his who was serving in the fleet which then guarded the Channel. A messenger had come from Namatius and, wrote Sidonius:

> He was quite certain that you had lately given the signal in your fleet and were on service, half military, half naval, coasting the shores of the ocean against the light, curved raiding vessels of the Saxons, in which you can reckon that however many of the crew you can see, so many brigands have you set eyes on. Those who command and those who obey, it is piracy they all teach and learn. So there is the greatest reason to warn you to be ever on the alert. It is an enemy more ferocious than any other.
>
> Unexpected he comes. If you are prepared he slips away. . . . Shipwrecks do not terrify the Saxons, such things are their exercise. The Saxons are not merely acquainted with the terrors of the sea, they are familiar with them.
>
> For since a storm, should there be one, puts us off our guard, the hope of a surprise attack leads them gladly to imperil their lives amid waves and broken rocks. Moreover, before they return to their country, setting sail from the Continent and dragging their anchors from the hostile shore, it is their custom to drown barbarously every tenth captive (such is their deplorable religion) casting equal lots over the doomed crowd. . . .

These were the people, ferocious, cruel, at home on the sea in all its moods and contemptuous of its dangers, who were soon to seize large areas of the former Roman province. The sea was no barrier to them but a pathway to loot and adventure. From their villages in Germany they sailed the grey waters of the North Sea and the Channel, ranging along the coasts of Gaul and south-eastern Britain. To begin with they fought no war and captured no territory. No political motives drove them on, nor any ambitions to win power or to change the frontiers of the Roman world. They were mere rovers in search of booty, thinking it shameful (as had been said of their ancestors three hundred years earlier) to earn by sweat what they could win by blood.[1] Their curved ships had for long been dreaded along the coasts of Britain. The British fleet had for a while held the island safe. But with the weakening of Roman power the raids of the Saxons increased and began to find a place in the chronicles. A Roman historian [2] tells us that about the year 365 the Saxons, together with the Picts and others, were harassing

[1] Tacitus, *Germania*.
[2] Ammianus, xxvi *et seq*.

Pewter chalice-like object from Ampleforth

Pewter bowl with Chi-Rho monogram on base, found at Ampleforth in association with the chalice-like object

Pewter ingot with Chi-Rho monogram

Stones from Kirkmadrine, Wigtownshire. On the right is the Florentius Stone

Britain continually. Three years later he reports that they were ravaging Gaul, invading by sea and by land, robbing and burning, and slaughtering all prisoners. They were feared more than any other enemies, he tells us in another passage, because of the suddenness of their raids.

Orosius, writing about 417, tells us that the Saxons were terrible enemies because of their bravery and their mobility.

The Roman mind had for centuries thought of the world as a land mass with an inner sea at the centre, and surrounded by the vast ocean. The roads which Rome built, and which remain as her sign manual, made travel by land an orderly and accustomed venture, with men moving safely along established routes from one secure city to another. But the sea they never mastered.

Now the Saxons were showing that a sailor had the width of the waters to range over. Each ship made its own road as it journeyed, leaving its white wake behind it as a swiftly fading mark of the brief path it had built. Wherever ship could float Saxon sword and shield could go.

By the middle of the fifth century it seemed to observers on the Continent that Britain was already lost to the Roman world and that she lay completely under the rule of the Saxon invaders.[1] This was not yet true, and the Britons were to make supreme efforts to save their island.

By 446 there seems to have been a lull in the activities of the Saxons, and the main danger at this time lay in the north. The Picts, now that the defences of Hadrian's Wall had finally been shattered, were invading the province continually. We have seen how in 429 they had joined forces with the Saxons. But now they were attacking alone. The attacks were unceasing and were made in force. The authorities in Britain, lacking trained troops and no doubt remembering the succour given to them by Germanus, decided once more to appeal for help to Rome. Aetius, a great commander, was for the third time consul in Rome. To him the Britons sent a desperate message. The Picts, they said, were driving them into the sea, and the sea was thrusting them back against the barbarians. They were faced with the grim alternative of having their throats cut on land or of drowning in the sea.[2] But no help came. Rome had her own preoccupations close at

[1] Prosper Tiro.

[2] Gildas, *De excidio Britanniae*, xx.

hand, and Aetius had battles to fight with barbarians nearer home, in Gaul and in Italy itself. There were no troops to spare to reinforce the defences of the island in the north.

The Britons, desperate for help and seeking any means that might enable them to hurl the Picts out of the province, remembered a method of obtaining reinforcements that had been successfully used by the Romans for many years. This was the enlisting of bodies of barbarian troops, transplanting them from their own country and giving them land within the Empire in return for military service. The whole arrangement was confirmed by a treaty under which the new troops were officered by their own chieftains. Because of this they were given the name of Treaty Troops, and many of them did good service.

Now that the Roman power had finally faded the Britons were again ruled by kings as they had been four hundred years before when the Romans first came. Chief among these kings was Vortigern. He was of course a Christian and was striving to maintain all that was left in the island of Roman forms and Roman civilization.

He it was who decided to establish a body of Treaty Troops in the province, with whose help he might defeat the Picts. For this purpose he selected the most warlike people he knew—the Saxons. A small number were invited into Britain under their leader Hengist, and they were given land in the Isle of Thanet off the coast of Kent.

At first this plan of Vortigern's was successful, and the Saxons inflicted heavy defeats upon their former allies the Picts. Soon, however, they realized that their military prowess could win them a better position than that of mere mercenaries fighting other men's battles.

Some nine years after their arrival the Saxon Treaty Troops were in open mutiny against King Vortigern. Two years later they fought another pitched battle and seized the whole of Kent. The Britons retreated into the walled city of London. Reinforcements came to the Saxons from Germany not only from the Saxon nation, but also from a neighbouring tribe called the Angles.[1] It was these last who ultimately were to give their name to the old Roman province which became known as Angleland or England.

But that lay in the future. The struggle for possession of the island

[1] *Anglo-Saxon Chronicle*, A.D. 455, 457.

was to be long and ferocious. Nor were the Britons ever totally defeated; they retained, and retain to this day, some corners of their old land.

Meantime Kent had gone, and the south-east promontory of the island was now firmly occupied by an alien and uncivilized people.

The Saxons and their allies the Angles lost nothing of their ferocity in their new home. Nor did they renounce their pagan religion. The beliefs of a conquered people normally have nothing to commend themselves to the conquerors. The gods of the Anglo-Saxons were warlike and savage personages more suited to their worship than the gentle God of love and forgiveness to whom the conquered Britons had vainly prayed. Therefore, as the tide of barbarism flowed darkly over the island, so with it spread the tide of paganism. At first in Kent and later throughout the wider regions occupied by the Anglo-Saxons the ancient churches grew deserted and derelict; the priests were silent, the bishops dethroned and the congregations dispersed.

We still remember the names of the Saxon gods, for it is the Saxon tongue that is now spoken in the island and their gods are commemorated in the names of the days of the week. There is the Moon, and the goddess Tiu, and Woden the all-powerful; there is Thor the god of thunder, Freya the goddess, Saturn and the Sun. Gradually these divinities spread their dominion. But the Britons strove mightily to uphold the cause of Christ and the cause of their nation. The two causes became one. The sorrow of the Britons was not merely that they were losing their land. They were affronted that it was a multitude of pagan barbarians that was destroying their civilization, their institutions and their ancient faith.

By now many monasteries had been established throughout Britain. In them the light of the Christian faith continued to shine. The prayers of the monks reinforced the strength of the soldiers. In spite of later traditions to the contrary British resistance was stubborn, effective and persistent. The Anglo-Saxons made no easy conquest of the old province.

Two or three hundred years later the English wrote down their own story of their long campaigns. The men who composed the document, known as the *Anglo-Saxon Chronicle*, must have relied for the most part upon spoken tradition, upon the songs and stories that were still sung and told of the coming of their ancestors and of the progenitors of their kings. Accuracy cannot be expected from such a work. Nevertheless the *Anglo-Saxon Chronicle* represents what the English believed to have happened. Where it errs, it probably errs in exaggerating their successes and minimizing their defeats. It is interesting therefore to trace the long slow story of their advance in the pages of the *Chronicle.*

The Saxons were summoned to Britain by King Vortigern as Treaty Troops in or about 446. They mutinied in 457 and swiftly seized the whole of Kent. Twenty years later landings were still being made by fresh invaders on the coast of Sussex. It was not until 491, thirty-four years after hostilities broke out, that they captured the old Roman fort at Pevensey. New parties are reported as coming over from Germany in 495 and 514. In 571 the *Chronicle* records the capture of Aylesbury one hundred and fourteen stubborn and weary years after the first conflict. Not until 577 did the Angles and Saxons capture the great cities of the south-west: Bath, Cirencester and Gloucester.[1] The grandsons and great-grandsons of those who had first fought against the pagan settlers were still fighting stubbornly, and for one and a quarter centuries the Britons had striven gallantly and obstinately to defend their Christian island. Nor was their entire land wrested from them. Wales they retained, safe in the high mountains and long green valleys, and Devon and Cornwall remained in their hands.

But the barbarians' advance, though slow, was inexorable. By the early 500's Britain was no longer the Christian island. Vast areas lay under the rule of the pagan Angles and Saxons who were now establishing their warlike kingdoms.

They knew nothing of Christianity and little of the island's past. Superstition, or perhaps awe, kept them away from the great walled cities of their predecessors. With few exceptions they built their own dwellings at some distance from the Roman towns, which fell into derelict and haunted ruins.

Their new farms were not built on the sites of the villas, and these too gradually fell into decay. The churches, with their long tradition of worship going back two centuries and more, lay desolate and silent. The painted wall plaster, gay with classical designs or Christian decorations, crumbled in the damp air of the roofless buildings. The milestones fell and the monuments, and the new settlers set up temples to their

[1] Bede, *Hist. Ecc.* i. 15.

ancient Gods; so that the name and knowledge of Christ faded from wide areas of the land.

Moreover the names of the Roman states, of the British kingdoms and of the tribes and peoples of Britain, were almost everywhere forgotten. The county of Kent retains the name of the Cantii, but for the most part the counties of southern and eastern England echo the names of the new kingdoms; the East Saxons, the South Saxons and the Middle Saxons are remembered in Essex, Sussex and Middlesex. The names of the great cities lived on long after they lay deserted and broken, but their names were distorted by English tongues. Every Roman town was a military camp in Saxon eyes. They therefore added the Latin word *castra* (a camp) in various guises to the now legendary names of the dead towns. *Venta* became Winchester and *Glevum* Gloucester.

By the great paved roads, now grass-grown and neglected, stood the timber farmhouses of the new people. Their ploughs cultivated the fields round the empty villas in the courtyards of which grew the tall trees, their roots undermining the walls. The frost of many winters crumbled the mortar from between the stones, and the stones themselves were carted away for the building of barn and byre. The English village replaced the Roman villa and rambling English towns the precise and planned Roman cities. And everywhere the worship of Odin and of Thor replaced the worship of Christ.

But beyond the reach of the tide of paganism Christianity lived on. And in the poems of the shattered British people and in the *Chronicle* of at least one British monk the great days of Britain, and the names of her heroes, were recorded and remembered.

5

THE SIXTH CENTURY

1

THE GROWING DARKNESS

WE HAVE seen the story of the long and laborious conquest of Britain as told by the English themselves in the *Anglo-Saxon Chronicle*. By good fortune we possess another account of the same long wars as seen through the eyes of the defeated and bewildered Britons.

In the year 517, somewhere in the north of the island, there was born a man named Gildas, who became known as Gildas the Wise.[1] We possess an account of his life said to have been written by Caradoc of Llancarfan. This appears to be of respectable age, but contains much that is clearly legendary rather than factual.

The *Life of St Gildas* tells us that Nau, King of Scotia and one of the most noble rulers in the north, had twenty-four sons. Gildas was one of these, and his parents decided that he should study literature. He proved a devoted and assiduous scholar. As a young man he crossed the sea to Gaul where he remained as a student for seven years. At the end of that time he returned to Britain, bringing with him a huge collection of books. His fame as a scholar was already widely known, and many pupils came from all parts of the island to study under him. He is then said to have lived a life of severe asceticism, fasting and praying, mixing his bread with ashes and—a conclusive sign of piety—never entering the baths to which his fellow Britons were thoroughly addicted! He was thin of face as if wasted by continuous fever. He would stand in the cold river at night praying, and continue his prayers in his cell until dawn. He slept little and then on hard stone with only one covering. He was, says his biographer, the most famous preacher and prophet throughout Britain, and even the kings feared him.

If any of this is true (and the style of Gildas's own writings suggests

[1] For the suggested dates of Gildas, see the present author's *Arthur: Roman Britain's Last Champion*, chapter xix.

that he was indeed a fierce and devoted man, with much of the fanatic in his make-up), we have a revealing picture of a Christian mystic in the sixth century. When we remember the zealous devotion of a man of this kind, who is described as outstanding but not unique, we can the better understand the resentment which the British Christians were to feel against Augustine, coming from Rome and claiming some special authority. The original inhabitants of the island that had produced a Gildas, and the monastic organization within which he worked, saw no need for any intruder from Rome to teach Christianity in their country.

Gildas was not only a deeply religious man, learned in the scriptures and seeking holiness through asceticism, he was also a deeply patriotic man, as harsh and unrelenting in his attitude towards the Saxon enemy and towards any Briton who weakened in the struggle as he was harsh and unrelenting in his conquest of his own earthly desires. Some time before 547, when he himself was in his late twenties, he wrote a brief history of Britain. In this book, *On the Destruction of Britain*, he is a contemporary of the later events described, and we can thus see the long and bitter war against the Saxons through British and Christian eyes.

He tells us of King Vortigern's planting of Saxon Treaty Troops a hundred years before his day. Because he had seen the appalling outcome he saw it not as a military and political act, but as a blind betrayal of the Christian faith. To invite the ferocious and unholy Saxons, hateful to God and men, and to seek their aid in fighting the Picts from the north, was to invite wolves into the sheepfold! He rails against the desperate and cruel darkness that had blinded the Britons to the certain consequences of their decision. 'How foolish are princes!' he exclaims, and draws a parallel from the Old Testament.[1] In his hysterical and hopeless outburst we can hear something of the anguish and despair of sixth-century Britain after a hundred years of bloody wars, still struggling against the heathen invader who now held so much of their land.

The first mutiny of the Treaty Troops he describes with vivid anger, seeing the assaults of the Saxons as similar to the attack of the Assyrians against Judaea. Again he quotes from the Old Testament: 'They have burned with fire the sanctuary; they have polluted on

[1] *De excid. Brit.* xxiii.

earth the tabernacle of Thy name.' He tells us of the destruction of buildings, of peaceful farmers put to flight, together with the leaders of the Church and the priests, 'while on every side weapons glitter and the flames crackle'.[1] We can see the horrors of the war, destroying the slow work of centuries. And we see it not merely as a war for territory; it is a life and death struggle for Christianity within the island. Amid the carnage and destruction he is as much concerned with the overthrow of holy altars as he is with the terrible loss of life.

In the next chapter he tells us of the successful revival of British resistance under a new leader, Ambrosius Aurelianus, who was descended (says Gildas) from parents who had 'worn the purple'. Under the leadership of his successors the Britons, 'though the virtues they inherited from their ancestors had now vastly degenerated', were at last victorious.[2]

Unfortunately he gives no dates for this British resurgence. But since he tells us that the progeny of Ambrosius was fighting at the time that he was writing (before 547), this means that Ambrosius had probably emerged as a leader towards the end of the fifth century.

Gildas's book ends on a strange and tantalizing note. He tells us that, after a period when sometimes the Saxons and sometimes the Britons were victorious, there was a final triumphant victory of the Britons ('the last but not the least massacre' of their pagan enemies). Gildas describes this engagement as the battle of Mount Badonicus. Where this hill was and what is its present name are matters now for speculation. But it was an outstanding and overwhelming victory for the Britons. It brought the invading Saxons to a halt. For a while British arms appeared to have achieved permanent success, and it at last seemed that the advance of the Saxons had been finally halted. Gildas tells us that a new golden age dawned for the Britons. Kings, magistrates, priests and citizens resumed their ancient tasks and duties. The triumph of British arms led to a revival of confidence and of order. The Christian faith was renewed and something of the old prosperity and happiness returned. The battle had been seen as a miracle, and men picked up the threads of their former lives with a sense of awe and thanksgiving. But, says Gildas, this did not last. One by one the generation that remembered the wonder of the battle died. The young,

[1] Ibid. xxv. [2] Ibid. xxvi.

ignorant of the terrible desolation of the earlier struggle, took present prosperity and peace for granted.

The narrative of Gildas is tantalizing because he tells us nothing of the events that led up to the battle. He does not name the commander who brought about this miraculous change in the fortunes of the Britons. Nor does he tell us the date of the great triumph. However, since he tells us that, by the time he was writing, a new generation had grown up who were ignorant of the stirring days of victory, we may assume that he was writing about thirty years after the battle. As his book was written before 547, a date of 517 can be taken for Mount Badonicus.

The account is equally tantalizing when Gildas turns to the events of his own day. He does not tell us precisely how the new generation of officials failed in their duty. He speaks of civil wars, but gives no details. He also tells us of men rushing headlong into hell and of our ancient mother, the Church (*venerabilis mater ecclesia*), overlooking those few who still reposed within her bosom as her only true children.

Yet the story is clear enough in outline: after Ambrosius Aurelianus there arose a leader among the British resolute and skilful enough to inflict an overwhelming defeat upon the terrible army of the Saxons. There was a period of peace and prosperity, lasting perhaps for thirty golden years, when the Saxons made no new advances, and when all the Britons, priests and laymen alike, resumed their ancient virtues and discharged fully the duties they owed to their triumphant nation. Then came civil war as the miracle of the battle was forgotten. And finally the Church itself was affected, so that even Gildas, the holy and selfless ascetic, could accuse the Church of having little regard for her true followers.

The resounding victory won by the Britons at Mount Badonicus is clearly an historic event, for it is mentioned not only by Gildas but also by another and independent chronicler. His name was Nennius, who wrote a brief *History of the Britons*. Unlike Gildas he was not a contemporary of the happenings about which he wrote. His book as it has come down to us was probably compiled about the year 800. However, it is based on much older material which may go back to within a hundred years or so of the period.

Immediately after recounting the story of St Patrick, Nennius tells us of the death of Hengist, the original leader of the Saxons, and of the coming to power of his son. At that time, he adds, the Saxons grew in strength and numbers, and increased in Britain. He goes on to recall that a man named Arthur was then fighting against the Saxons on the side of the various kings of the Britons. Arthur is not described as a king but as *Dux bellorum*, or leader of the wars.[1] Nennius then lists twelve battles in which this leader was victorious. And the twelfth, he tells us, was the battle of Mount Badon in which there perished on one day nine hundred and sixty men in one single charge of Arthur's. For no one else laid them low but only he himself, acting alone.

This is of course the Arthur around whose name numerous myths and legends were to gather in later years. The strength of those legends is an indication of the tremendous reputation that he must have enjoyed throughout Britain long after the Saxons had finally conquered, and when the hopes engendered by his overwhelming victory had perished in the days of final defeat.

Perhaps the most striking feature in the narrative of Nennius is his description of the part played by Christianity in the stubborn resistance of the Britons. For in his account of the eighth battle he tells us that Arthur bore an image of St Mary the Virgin. On that day the pagans were put to flight and 'there was great slaughter among them through the power of Our Lord Jesus Christ and through the power of St Mary the Virgin, His Mother'. William of Malmesbury, a later writer, repeats this.[2]

In another chronicle [3] we are told that Arthur 'carried the cross of Our Lord Jesus Christ' at the battle of Badon.

Evidently the commander of the armies of Britain was seen, and was still seen in later ages, as a Christian champion, leading the forces of Christianity against the pagan invaders. The idea of a nation-state had not yet been born. The armies of Britain were not, therefore, fighting for the abstraction of Britain or for the British nation. They were fighting for survival and for the survival of the Christian religion. They saw their commander not merely as a leader of the Britons but as a leader of Christian citizens in their long struggle with the pagan invaders.

The fact that Gildas, while recording the name of Ambrosius

[1] Nennius, *Hist. Brit.* 56.
[2] William of Malmesbury, I. i.
[3] *Annales Cambriae*, entry for 416.

Aurelianus, does not name the victor of the famous battle suggests that he himself was unfriendly towards that great commander. Some hint of the truth is to be found in the biography of Gildas at which we have already glanced. In it we are told that Gildas was a contemporary of one, Arthur, King of all Great Britain, whom he greatly loved and whom he always sought to obey. But his twenty-three brothers opposed this 'rebel king', being unwilling to endure his rule. One of the brothers, Hueil, 'a devoted warrior and most famous soldier', would give obedience to no king, not even to this man Arthur. He would often sally out of Scotia on foray, burning and ravaging in search of booty. He won great acclaim and was spoken of as a future king. Arthur, King of the whole of Britain, attacked and slew him, rejoicing that he had killed his most powerful enemy. Gildas himself was in Ireland at the time, teaching in Armagh. When he heard of his brother's death he wept bitterly. Formerly he had prayed for Arthur, now his brother's persecutor and executioner. Thenceforward he prayed every day for the soul of his dead brother.

In the story of Hueil we have a glimpse of the civil wars with which Britain was torn. Moreover the story would explain why Gildas was silent as to the name of the British commander who won the miraculous victory. He could not praise the name of his brother's murderer.

The biographer tells of a happy ending. Gildas returned out of Ireland to his own land, bringing a beautiful and most sweet-sounding bell as an offering to the Church. He was received by the abbot of Llancarfan. When news of his return spread all the leading bishops and abbots throughout Britain flocked to him. Arthur also came. Gildas forgave him for his brother's death, kissed him and gave him his blessing. Arthur wept and the two men were reconciled.

After visiting Rome Gildas is said to have resided at Glastonbury, which was besieged by Arthur. Later he built a church close by where he ended his days in prayer and fasting, honoured throughout the land.

In addition to his book *On the Destruction of Britain* Gildas wrote a much longer work known as *The Epistle*, which again shows us something of the stresses and quarrels that were dividing the Britons. For in it Gildas records all the evil that he saw among the kings and other authorities of Britain. He is evidently telling us of the situation when the golden age was over, and when the afterglow of the miraculous victory had faded.

Darkness is gathering over the British nation; it is the darkness of despair, of disunity and of imminent total defeat. The kings are not kings but tyrants. Prisons are filled not through the judgments of justice but by treachery. Men are murdered within the sanctuary of churches and the bloody garments of the murderers brush against the altar raised to receive the sacred Body of God. Adultery, incest, lust and sodomy are ascribed to the kings. The prophets of the Old Testament and the Epistles of St Paul are quoted at length by Gildas in his denunciation of present crimes and his summons to past virtues.

The total picture is one of gloom. After a hundred years of resolution, of fighting on with enduring will, the Britons were ceasing to be a nation and were breaking up into separate kingdoms ruled by selfish and ambitious kings. There were still men like Gildas soaked in and devoted to the Christian faith; men who saw the chaos of a war-stricken land as an obscene insult to the holiness of God's purpose. There were men to whom the words of Isaiah and of Paul were, through a lifetime of reading, as familiar as the voices of their own close friends. But these men were few and were growing fewer. The great prelates of the Church ignored them, and the kings, although they feared them, gave no heed to their exhortations. With their spirit at last weakened by the long wars, with their faith in Christianity growing dim in the darkness of war and defeat, the Britons were nearing the end of their story.

Their endurance in the face of cruelty, bloodshed and destruction had been almost unbelievable. For a hundred years and more they had fought a determined and pitiless enemy. They had been forced in innumerable battles to retreat across nearly the whole width of their island. They had kept hope alive when all things taught despair. They had kept their western lands free from their enemies for a hundred and twenty years. Their armies had starved in forest and heathland. Refugees had died and their enemies had exulted. Their faith and their religion had stood, tall rocks on a shelving beach, standing with stubborn pride above the waters long after the whole shore had been engulfed. But now even their unimaginable courage could no longer hold out. In despair they quarrelled among themselves. Kings fought one another for the illusion of power in a land within which all power would shortly pass to alien hands. The story of Britain was nearly over, reaching no heroic climax, but ending in a pitiful squandering of the last few remnants of its strength in recrimination and civil war. And the history of England was beginning.

2

THE ENDURING FAITH

Although wide areas of the old Roman province were, by the sixth century, fully in the hands of the pagan invaders, the Christian faith continued to flourish in those parts of the land that were still held by the Britons. Almost their last refuge was the high mountain country west of the Wye. Here, in what is now Wales, the Britons stubbornly lived their own lives for many centuries, waging continued war, sometimes offensive and sometimes defensive, against the Saxons on their borders. Here they kept alive their ancient Christian tradition; here in song and in legend they recorded the heroism of their leaders and the bravery of their fighting men. It was to be five hundred years and more before they were to be finally subjugated. Even then, though the conquest was final it was never total; so that to this day the old British tongue (with its many Latin words that are an enduring memorial to the great days of the Roman island) is still spoken, and the pride of the Britons still endures in the hills and valleys of Wales. It was in Wales therefore, when almost all the rest of the province had fallen to the Saxons, that Christianity continued to flourish. And it was in this last stronghold of the Christian Britons that new saints arose, even in the dark days of the sixth century.

In the town of Old Menevia in Glamorganshire, known to the Romans as *Vetus Menevia* and to the Welsh as Hen Mynw, there lived a nobleman named Sanctus, of which name the Welsh form is Sandde. His father's name was Ceredig, his mother's Non; his grandfather was Cunedda. The family was Christian, and when a son was born in the first years of the sixth century he was baptized by Albeus, Bishop of Munster, in Ireland, who was at that time visiting Britain.

The Cirencester Word Square, engraved on a fragment of wall plaster

The Icklingham 'Font'

The boy was given the Christian name David. Some five hundred years later an account of his life was written by one of his successors to the see which he had founded.[1]

David is said to have been educated by St Paulinus at Whitland in Carmarthenshire; and Paulinus was yet another pupil of St Germanus.

At some date which cannot be ascertained David founded a monastery near his birthplace in the valley of the Ross. He himself became abbot, and that position, in accordance with the custom of the times, gave him the rank of bishop. Here he lived for many years in tranquillity, supervising the building of church and monastery and organizing his new society. Though his life was quiet and withdrawn, his reputation for scholarship and wisdom grew in the outside world.

When the heresy of Pelagius began to spread into Wales it caused serious concern to Dubricius (St Dyfrig), who occupied the archiepiscopal see, at that time situated at Caerleon-on-Usk, the old headquarters of the Second Legion. Dubricius accordingly summoned a synod of bishops to meet at Llandewi-Brefi to develop arguments against the heresy and to decide upon steps to combat it. David, holding the rank of bishop, was ordered with the rest to attend. His biographer says he was most reluctant to go; his vocation, he felt, lay in the studious quiet of his monastery rather than in the disputatious strife of theology and ecclesiastical politics. He had to be virtually dragged to the assembly.

Once there, however, he played an outstanding part in the discussions. He proved not merely eloquent—eloquence was perhaps a not uncommon quality in that part of the country—but also learned and reasonable. Dubricius, who was now getting on in years, realized that in David he had found an ideal successor. Moulded by the same influences as himself, a scholar who had not ceased to be a student, a practical organizer (as his new monastery witnessed), eloquent yet moderate in council, David would obviously fill the high office with distinction and would protect, in those difficult and perilous times, the cause of British Christianity. Dubricius acted swiftly upon the decision he had taken. He resigned his office, having first nominated David as his successor, and David was forthwith appointed.

[1] Rhygyvarch (died 1099) one of the last British bishops of St Davids. His *Life* was edited with translation by A. W. Wade-Evans, 1914. From that work Giraldus Cambrensis compiled another biography, full of absurdities.

That is one story. Another states that after the Synod of Llandewi-Brefi he went on pilgrimage to Jerusalem, and was there consecrated bishop with metropolitan jurisdiction over South Wales. The true facts cannot now be discovered. We know, however, that as primate he presided over the so-called Synod of Victory at Caerleon, and that later still he moved the seat of ecclesiastical government from there to the headland of Mynyw or Menevia, which is still, under the name St David's (*Ty-Dwei* = House of David), an episcopal city.

The second synod provides us with a point of reference in dating the events of David's life. Appended to one of the manuscripts of the work of Nennius is a brief Welsh Chronicle, known as the *Annales Cambriae*. Although the manuscript is not earlier than the eleventh century, these annals incorporate older material. The entries seem reliable, for when they can be checked against other sources they appear to be accurate. Against the year 569 is the entry: *Synodus Victoriae apud Britones congregatur*—'The Synod of Victory was assembled among the Britons'. So David was appointed bishop some fifty-two years after the victory of Badon, and long after the ephemeral golden age, described by Gildas, had faded. By now Saxon kingdoms had been firmly established in the old province. Indeed the Saxons were now turning their swords against one another. Confident that the island was their own, they were contending with one another for power and for the overlordship of their new land.[1]

Thus David's see was now of supreme importance. In former days the archbishop had been a local leader, eminent certainly and bearing great responsibilities, but of purely local significance. Now the primacy was an office within the vital heartland of the British people and of British Christianity. Britons lived on in the new Saxon territories, but at best as defeated and dejected men, and at worst as slaves. Only in Wales and in the western territories of the island did they live as a nation.

David therefore became the leader and guardian of the Christian faith. These responsibilities he discharged faithfully and with success, so that his work was long remembered in legend, and he himself became St David of Wales, patron saint of the surviving Britons.

According to the *Annales Cambriae*, St David died in 601; he must then have been in extreme old age. He founded numerous churches

[1] *Anglo-Saxon Chronicle*, A.D. 568.

throughout his archdiocese, and no fewer than fifty-three continue to preserve his name. His shrine at St David's became a famous centre of pilgrimage, and at the request of King Henry I he was formally canonized by Pope Calixtus II about 1120. It was due to St David, and to others like him whose names are not recorded, that the Christian faith of the Britons survived their military overthrow, and that the religion which had been so long rooted in the island continued to grow and to flower—at least in places—after the political and social structure of Roman Britain, within which it was first planted, had been overwhelmed and destroyed.

We have faint glimpses of another bishop of those dark days. Teilo was born at Penally, near Tenby in Pembrokeshire. Educated by St Dyfrig, he was a companion (some say a cousin) of St David. Following the example of others, he founded a monastery and school near Llandaff in Carmarthenshire, of which he himself was abbot-bishop.

Towards the middle of the sixth century there was a widespread outbreak of plague. The epidemic started in western Asia and had reached south-eastern Europe by the 540's. A little later it reached Britain. According to the *Annales Cambriae* it was rife in the island in 547, for King Maglocunus is reported as dying in that year 'of the great mortality'. When the plague struck Wales Teilo left the island and took refuge in Armorica, where he was received with honour. There he must have learned of the disastrous state of affairs in Britain as the Saxon power extended, for Gildas tells us that many Britons, in the days of their defeat, 'crossed the seas with loud lamentations'.[1]

At the end of seven years, about 554, Teilo returned to his homeland. Undeterred by tales of defeat and desolation, he took ship for Cornwall and thence travelled back to Llandaff. If his death took place, as commonly believed, *circa* 580, we may dismiss the statement of some hagiographers that he succeeded St David.

The Britons who dwelt in Wales devised a verse form called the Triad. In the Triads are celebrated the nation's saints and heroes, grouped in threes. Teilo is honoured twice in these poems. He is listed as one of the three canonized saints of the island of Britain. (The Latin tongue had now decayed and *Insula Britanniae* has become *Ynis Pritain* in the Triads, but pride in the island and its past had outlived the classical language in which her glories had been wrought.) He is

[1] *De excid. Brit.* xxv.

commemorated a second time as one of the three holy visitors to *Ynis Pritain*, recalling his homeward journey from safe refuge in Armorica to the ardours and dangers of the darkening island.

3

THE HOLY ISLE

DURING this period there came to Britain from overseas another man who was to leave his mark on the island's Christian story. Unlike his predecessors, he did not come from the continent of Europe but from Ireland. The work of St Patrick had endured there and the faith and learning which he had planted were now flourishing. Ireland repaid her debt to Britain, birthplace of St Patrick, through the missionary work of St Columba who came to Britain in the mid sixth century and who continued the work of St Ninian among the northern tribes.

Columba was born at Garton in Donegal in or about the year 521. Through his father, Conal Gulban, he was descended from the piratical King Niall of the Nine Hostages. He studied first under St Finian at Moville, near the head of Strangford Lough, and then under Finian's more famous namesake at Clonard. He began his monastic life at Glasnevin, and at once embarked on his apostolate. He had already founded the monasteries of Derry (545) and Durrow (*circa* 550) when he was ordained priest about 551.

After twelve more years of work in Ireland Columba took ship, crossed over to northern Britain, and on Whitsun Eve 563 landed with twelve companions in the kingdom of the Picts. The local king, Bridius, received him kindly, allowed him to preach and to make converts among the people and bestowed upon him the small island of Iona off the west coast of Argyllshire. Here he established the greatest and most celebrated of all his foundations, which soon proved to be the strongest factor in the conversion of Picts, Scots and northern English.

Columba travelled widely. He made long journeys on the mainland, through the wild highlands as far north as Aberdeen, and it is said that within thirty years he had converted all northern Scotland. He often revisited Ireland, attending synods there, and Iona thus became a link between the Christians of Scotland and of Ireland, and occupied a central place in the Celtic Church.

One Saturday afternoon in 597 Columba, at the age of seventy-six, sat working on a copy of the Psalm 'They who seek the Lord . . .'. His hand grew tired and he laid down his pen saying: 'Brother Barthen will have to write the rest.' He attended Vespers and returned to his cell. He rose after a few hours' rest and was the first to reach the church for Matins. When the monks filed in a few moments later they found him stretched out before the altar. They hurried to help him, but he died where he lay, a smile upon his face. A life that had begun in turmoil had ended in tranquillity.

St Adamnan, abbot of Iona in 679, wrote a life of his great predecessor,[1] in which occur these famous words: 'He had the face of an angel; he was of an excellent nature, polished in speech, holy in deed, great in counsel . . . loving unto all.'

The year of Columba's death was the year of Augustine's arrival. News of the death of yet another of the island's saints would have reached the Britons in the south almost at the same time that they heard of the landing of the mission from Rome.

4

THE HEATHEN KINGDOMS

ALL this while, when the Britons were being pushed westwards and when their ancient social and political order was crumbling, with Christianity as almost the only bond that might still hold them together,

[1] Adamnan's *Life* is an enlargement of an earlier biography by Abbot Cuminius of Iona, *c.* 657.

the pagan invaders were consolidating the territories they had won, and were founding their many kingdoms.

The struggle had long ceased to be a simple mutiny of Treaty Troops or the mere seizing of land by Saxons already in the island. News of the Saxons' first successes was carried back to their homeland, with tempting descriptions of rich green farmlands to be bought with a brief battle. Tales of the dwindling of effective resistance by the Britons, and of the latters' armies in disarray, were heard with delight in the crowded lands of northern Germany. New adventurers loaded their ships with arms and provisions and sailed across the forbidding waves of the North Sea to make landfall along the east coast of Britain. These new invaders were no longer pirates seeking easy plunder and a swift return to their own homes. They were coming to seize farmland and sea-haven, to build their own new country on the defenceless soil of the old Roman province. Their leaders sought more than land for hunting and harvest. They hoped to carve out their own kingdoms and to exchange the oar-bench for the throne, to build their own great halls from the oak of the island's forests, and to wear the rich gold of her mines. In their own country east of the Rhine they had never come under the rule of Rome. They knew nothing of magistrate and consul, of tribune or prefect. Their societies were built around a military leader, a king, who was the centre and commander of a body of fighting men. These followed him in battle and these he protected and rewarded in times of peace. It was considered a disgrace for these men to survive their chief in battle. He in turn accounted it his duty to win booty in war with which to reward them.

It was devoted and resolute war bands of this kind, led by equally resolute and battle-eager kings, that now came on their ambitious adventures. One by one the leaders set up their kingdoms in Britain, rewarding their followers with broad acres of rich farmland and stolen treasure.

First of these was the kingdom of Kent, where the Saxon Treaty Troops had originally been settled. When Hengist, their original leader, died his son succeeded him and reigned as king for twenty-four years. Perhaps because the Saxons had been granted this land peacefully, and had not taken it by conquest nor by the enslavement or slaughter of the local inhabitants,[1] they did not name the new kingdom

[1] Nennius, *Hist. Brit.* xxxvii.

after their own people; they named it after the Britons who dwelt there, the Cantii. So it became the kingdom of Kent and the name survives to this day. Aesc, Hengist's son, became king in 488,[1] and the kingdom of Kent may be said to date from that time.

Thirty-one years later, in 519, the kingdom of the West Saxons (Wessex) was established under Cerdic. He and his son had come to the island with five ships in 495, so that it had taken him twenty-four years to win royal state. His kingdom grew and prospered. The West Saxons became the spearhead of the pagan advance against the Britons. King Cerdic may well have been among those opposed to the Britons at Mount Badon. If so, then he was defeated but not overthrown. Maybe it was to renew their strength after the disaster to their arms at Badon that the West Saxons, two years later, acclaimed Cerdic as their king. By 552, when the thirty years of Gildas's golden age were over, Cerdic's son Cynric had fought his way westwards as far as Salisbury and had there put the Britons to flight.

Now, behind the western fighting line, in the secure Saxon lands where the kingdoms of Kent and Wessex watched uneasily the growth of one another's power, the two states began to war against each other. In 568 Ceawlin, King of Wessex, fought with Aethilberht and drove him back into Kent.

The third of the great kingdoms to be set up lay north of the River Humber. Bede [2] tells us that Ida began to rule in Northumbria in 547 and reigned for twelve years. Like the kingdom of Wessex in the south, Northumbria had not been set up by the forward thrust of barbarians already in the island, but by new waves of invaders coming across the North Sea. This kingdom was to grow into one of the most powerful and warlike of the new states. By the early seventh century its king, Aethilfrid, was devastating the lands of the Britons more than any other English prince.[3]

It is now proper to speak of the English rather than separately of the Angles and of the Saxons. Although the name 'Saxons' was indiscriminately applied by the Britons to all invaders from Germany, it was the name of their neighbours the Angles which was ultimately to be given to the whole people and to the land where they now dwelt. Hengist, who is recorded by British chroniclers as a leader of the

[1] *Anglo-Saxon Chronicle.* [2] *Hist. Ecc.* v. 24.
[3] *Hist. Ecc.* i. 35.

Saxon Treaty Troops, might himself have been an Angle. For Nennius speaks of Hengist as having consulted with his elders '*qui venerant secum de insula Oghgul*', that is to say with his elders who had come with him from the island of Oghgul. This has been taken by some to mean Angle, and the phrase may be a hint that Hengist and his elders had come from the land of the Angles and were of that tribe. In later years the Angles and Saxons themselves made no clear distinction between their two peoples, but used both names for either folk. Generally their enemies continued to call them Saxons. The Englishman is to this day a Sassenach, or Sassenaeg, as far as his Scottish and Welsh neighbours are concerned. Gradually, however, the name Angle replaced 'Saxon' in the language of the Anglo-Saxons themselves. So they became the Angli or the English.

Many Britons lived on in the new Saxon kingdoms, for not all had fled into the western lands. The poorer farmers clung as long as they could to their fields and cottages, while some of the rich and powerful also remained. For chronicles of the kings of Northumbria, like those of the kings of Wessex, contain many Celtic names. This suggests that kings and princes of the new Saxon states sometimes intermarried with the old British population. Many place names of villages in the eastern parts of England also suggest that numbers of the Britons lived on in the new kingdoms. Often their victors enslaved them and gave them the derisory name *Wealas* or foreigners. Village names like Walbrook and Walton, and the name of the principality of Wales itself, are memorials to the defeat and humiliation of the Britons.

Later came the kingdom of Mercia, the land of the Marches that lay on the frontier of the territories of the Britons. At first it was a dependant of Northumbria, but became an independent and powerful force under its great king Penda. He traced his proud descent from the god Woden and was one of the greatest of the pagan leaders of the seventh century. But he made an alliance with the Christian Britons against his fellow pagans when it was necessary to enlarge his power or extend his dominions,[1] and he is remembered by chroniclers of the Britons as well as of the Saxons.

Also in the north was the kingdom of Deira, part of the Northumbrian lands and, like Mercia, a latecomer among the new states. It lay

[1] Tigernach, *Annales*, A.D. 631.

on the north-east coast, from Darlington southwards to the Humber, extending inland to York and to the rivers Swale and Ouse. It was a group of young men from this northern kingdom that awakened the interest of a Roman priest in the strange, fair inhabitants of the lost province of Britain.

But this lay in the future. Throughout the sixth century all the new kingdoms were solidly pagan. They had adopted none of the religion of the folk they had conquered, but still worshipped the old gods of their homeland. Many of their kings, such as Penda of Mercia, claimed descent from Woden. Of the formal rites and ceremonial of their religion we know little. Of the general shape of their beliefs and of the spirit which infused them we know a great deal from their poems and legends. This world was a harsh place of ice and snow. The cold grain of hail fell on a grey and unrelenting sea. Strange monsters peopled the earth, and stole out of the darkness of night when men lay sleeping in the hall; and the monsters crept stealthily into the dwellings of men and would snatch a warrior silently from among his companions as he lay stretched out on the bench, drowsy with feasting and with beer. The gods did not intervene in the affairs of man, and it was of little use to plead with them. A man's fate was fixed. Those who were destined to die in battle would die, and those who were to survive would do so. A man could but follow the code which governed a soldier's behaviour and leave the outcome to destiny. There was great joy in battle, when the arrows hissed like angry snakes, and the chain mail of the byrnies sang aloud to the blows of the foeman's sword. Spears stung and men died if it was their weird to die. And the raven came to the field and the wolf, that grey beast, to devour the unlucky. When cattle ailed or crops withered a spell could help to set matters right. A charm in verse, a song sung at the right time, and the cattle would recover and the fields grow fertile. There were charms for evil too, and a man might be bewitched and enchanted within the four walls of a mortal house, but was safe from magic under the open sky. In springtime came the celebrations of the goddess Eostre, with eggs to bring fertility to the new harvest and hot buns to recall the stored grain of last year's growth. At midwinter came the festival of Yule, and much rejoicing that the light days were coming and that the ice and snow would give way to the advancing sun. Then there were feasting and drinking and making merry with good meat and full cup. Some of their gods, so Bede tells us, required the sacrifice of an ox, whose flesh was eaten for the glory of the god and the pleasure of men's stomachs. (The English were always great eaters of beef!) Their world was a world of winter and of battle, of keen sorrow and rough pleasure; the Anglo-Saxons were inured to hardship and resigned to suffering.

This harsh world, cold with wind and frost, made loud with the sound of battle or quiet with the tranquillity of death, was far removed from the world of the Christian Britons, and utterly alien to their solemn churches and quiet monasteries. The Britons could see no possible way of reconciling these two ways of life which were so remote from one another, and whose followers, although they shared an island, seemed to live in two separate worlds that had no dimension in common and no meeting point.

5

THE GROWING ISOLATION

THE Britons, now as a nation confined to the mountainous land of Wales and to the south-western peninsula of Devon and Cornwall, with their once proud cities in the rest of the island fallen into forgotten and squalid ruins, kept their Christian faith alive in their diminished territory. Their bishops still led the people; in church and monastery Mass was still celebrated and the old learning still husbanded in the austere cells of monks. But as the fabric of the social order grew tattered and decayed, with many kings contending with one another for power instead of striving in unity against the common enemy, so did the unity and simplicity of the Church begin to wear away.

Gildas, writing in or after 547, found it in his heart to rail against some of his fellow priests with angry vehemence. Britain had priests, he says, but they were foolish; many who ministered, but they were shameless; she had clerks, but they were cheating plunderers. Britain had shepherds, but they were wolves, ready for the slaughter of the souls of their flocks.[1] The Church of Britain, like the defence of Britain, was in disarray. Gildas of course may have been exaggerating and his pen may well have been guided by the bitterness of defeat. What is certainly true is that the Britons made no recorded attempt to convert the new heathen population to Christianity. The sixth century produced no Patrick and no Ninian to travel into the lands of the barbarians and to bring them the news of Christ. Bede, who was writing only two hundred years later, and who in this context was drawing on Gildas for information, counts it one of the Briton's most unspeakable crimes that they never preached the Christian faith to the Saxons who now lived in the same island.[2] He adds, with solid contempt for the conquered people, that God later sent worthier men to teach the truth to the English people!

It is true that Christianity preaches forgiveness and that every Christian daily prays that he may be forgiven as he forgives those who have sinned against him. But it was asking a great deal of the Britons to expect them to go out into the lands of their enemies and to try to bring to God those ferocious and persistent foes who had invaded their territory, had destroyed their way of life and had slaughtered or enslaved so many of their kin. If Bede, a scholarly and moderate man, could allow contempt and scorn to enter his heart when mentioning the Britons two hundred years after the first phase of the struggle, we can imagine the bitterness that stood between the two nations during the early years of contention. Thus any comparison between the failure of the Britons to send missionaries to the Saxons with their earlier missions to other barbarian peoples is misleading. For though the Scots had kept Patrick in bondage they had acted according to their lights in a society where slavery was acceptable. The Picts had not wronged Ninian nor harmed his people. For those earlier saints the task of a missionary was acceptable and challenging. It was quite otherwise for the beaten and deprived Britons. The judgment of Bede sounds harsh against the background of fire and slaughter which Gildas has recorded. More than human virtue would have been required for men to go out and teach the destroyers of their society and the slayers of their people. The priests of Britain did not venture into the new lands of England, but remained among their own people, withdrawing into

[1] Gildas, *Ep.* lxvii. [2] *Hist. Ecc.* i. 22.

the peaceful monasteries of Wales and preaching in the churches of their diminished homeland.

Gradually they grew remote from the mainstream of Christianity on the Continent. The regularity of their contacts with the bishops in Gaul faltered and fell away. In 455, for example, Pope Leo had ordered a modification of the methods used in calculating the date of Easter. Britain was then still in communication with Rome, and news of the changes was sent to the British churches. During the next fifty years a further alteration was made. But the new instructions never reached the island, and Christians in Britain continued for nearly a century to celebrate the Resurrection at a date different from that used by their fellow Christians on the Continent. No longer did bishops from Britain travel to Gaul to attend conferences at Arles and elsewhere as they had done so frequently in happier days. No longer did visiting bishop or priest come from Gaul into Britain to give counsel and aid to the citizens of the island.

Because of this isolation, Christians in Britain ceased over the years to look to Rome as the head and centre of their faith. Throughout the Continent the power and standing of the Bishop of Rome were growing. But in Britain, by the late sixth century, he appears to have occupied no special place in the minds of the British bishops and priests. They saw themselves as the sole repository of truth, ringed by barbarian lands and certain that, with their long and venerable Christian traditions and with the Scriptures in their hands, they could continue unaided to tread the path of true teaching and correct doctrine. By the end of the century, unburdened by any belief in the special authority of the Pope, they would not hesitate to reject one of his special legates.

6

THE PLANNING OF A MISSION

GILDAS was able to recall with pride that his country had ceased to be called Britain and had become known as the Roman island.[1] Fifty years later all that was changed. Just as Rome had grown remote and far from the Christian Britons, so had the island of Britain faded from the knowledge of people in Rome and in the lands of the continental Empire. As in the days of Caesar, some six hundred years before, so now Britain had become to Roman eyes a mysterious and unknown land lying on the very edge of the world. It became an almost legendary country of which strange and eerie stories were told. Procopius, writing in Constantinople at about the same time that Gildas was composing his mournful book in Britain, records that the island was a place to which the souls of the dead were ferried from the shores of the Continent across the Channel. He described the lands that lay north of the Wall as deserts in which serpents dwelt, and where the air was so foul that no man could survive there for half an hour.

As in so many legends, fact mingles with fiction in his narrative. For he records that three large nations lived in the island of Britain. He tells us that the names of these people were the *Angili*, the *Phrissones* and the *Brittones*, the last of which had taken their name from the island. These names were as near as Procopius could get to the names of the Angles, the Frisians and the Britons. He knew that there was a separation of the nations in the island, for he tells us that each of these people was ruled over by their own king. This mixture of fact and fantasy shows how scant was the knowledge of Britain an the Continent. In Rome itself the situation was much the same. It was known that the island had fallen to a barbarous, warlike and pagan nation, whose language was unknown to the civilized world. These rumours and the terrifying reputation of the island's ferocious new inhabitants discouraged travellers from crossing the Channel. For nearly five

[1] *De excid. Brit.* vii.

hundred years Rome and Britain had been in continuous and intimate communication. Now the last links were broken and it was as if the close ties had never been.

For centuries the people of Britain had profited by their contacts with Rome, through which they had shared in the benefits of European civilization. The people of England were now in grave danger of isolation and of remaining in the darkness of perpetual barbarism, unrelieved by any light from the outer world.

The event which was to change the destiny of England, bringing the island once more under the influence of Rome, was of itself trivial enough. Gregory, famous in history as St Gregory the Great, was born in Rome *circa* A.D. 540. At the age of about thirty-five he became a monk and one of the city's seven regional deacons. Some four years later Pope Pelagius II appointed him his representative at Constantinople. There he remained until about 586, when he was appointed by the same Pope abbot of the monastery of St Andrew of the Caelian hill.

Not long afterwards Gregory heard that there had arrived in Rome a group of Saxons from the island of Britain.[1] His curiosity was at once aroused. If in Constantinople he had heard some of the strange stories which Procopius had recorded, it is easy to understand the interest which these visitors awakened in him. Gregory desired to see them. The party consisted of a group of handsome boys; some say that they were in fact young men of striking beauty and with fair curly hair. They were Angles and they came from the northern kingdom of Deira that lay round the once great military city of York. Their king at this time was called Aelle.

It is said that Gregory gazed with admiration on their fair good looks and asked the name of their nation. He was told that the people from whom they came were called Angles (*Angli*). He said: 'Not Angles, but angels' (*Non Angli sed angeli*). He next asked the name of their king. And to the answer 'Aelle', he replied: '*Alleluia*, for there ought the praise of the Lord to be!' Finally he asked the name of the region from which they came. 'Deira', he was told. He answered: '*De ira Dei*—from the wrath of God, fleeing to the faith!'

The impression made upon Gregory was a deep and lasting one. Some time was to elapse before he could put into operation the plan

[1] Bede, *Hist. Ecc.* ii. 1 says they had been brought for sale as slaves.

which the incident had prompted in his mind. For the present, he asked the Pope that a mission might be sent to the country of the English to convert them to Christianity. He said it was a dreadful thing that Hell should be peopled by folk of such beauty. Pelagius gave him permission to go to Britain himself. But Gregory was immensely popular in Rome, and many were reluctant for him to leave the city. Demonstrations were organized, and the Sovereign Pontiff was greeted with shouts on his way to St Peter's Church. The demonstrators called out: 'You have offended Peter; you have destroyed Rome; you have dismissed Gregory!' Pelagius withdrew his permission and ordered Gregory to remain in Rome. About a hundred and fifty years later this tale was written down by a monk of Whitby.[1]

In 590 Pelagius II died and Gregory was chosen to succeed him. Five years later we find him writing a letter to a priest named Candidus who was setting out on a journey into Gaul: 'We wish you to buy clothing for the poor, or for English boys of the age of seventeen and eighteen, that they may be dedicated to the service of God and educated in monasteries.'[2] It is interesting that he defines fairly closely the age of the English boys to whom Candidus was to play the benefactor. It may be that the Angles whom he had seen in Rome had been lads of about that age.

Because all communications between Rome and Britain had now virtually ceased, Gregory was unaware that the first contacts with Christianity, albeit indirect, were already being made by the fair-haired inhabitants of the old province. King Aethilberht of Kent had married a princess from Gaul named Bertha. She was from the kingdom of the Franks and was a Christian. Her parents had given her permission to wed the pagan king on condition that she would be allowed to continue in her religion. She came to Kent accompanied by her own bishop, Liudhard.

In King Aethilberht's capital city of Canterbury there was an old church, built by the Britons in the prosperous Roman days and dedicated to St Martin. It had long lain derelict and deserted. Now, at the king's orders, it was cleaned and restored for Queen Bertha's worship.[3] After over a hundred years of silence, the ancient building was once

[1] *Vita Sancti Gregorii*, quoted by R. W. Chambers in *England Before the Conquest*.

[2] R. W. Chambers, op. cit. [3] Bede, *Hist. Ecc.* i. 24.

more the scene of Christian ceremonies. Christian prayers and the words of the gospels were again heard in the lost land that had been granted by Vortigern to the pagan Saxons; and they were heard in a building that had been erected by the Britons, whose handiwork was thus enduring more successfully than they had dared to hope in the hour of their defeat.

But Gregory knew nothing of this during the years when he dreamed his dream of converting the pagan English to the worship of Christ. Patiently, and with his resolve undiminished by time, he awaited his opportunity.

7

ROME RETURNS

IT WAS not, however, until several years after his election to the papacy that Gregory I was ready to dispatch the expedition he had long meditated. He chose as its leader a man named Augustine, who was the Prior of St Andrew's, his old monastic home. The mission was organized and ready to leave by 596. The party was a large one, consisting of about forty monks. We know the names of some—Laurentius (a priest) and Peter. They set out for Britain in the early summer, travelling through the Italian countryside in June or July under the hot and golden sun. But the high hopes with which they started their journey soon evaporated. Each day's travel brought home to them the dangers of their enterprise. They had gone out a short way when the full realization of its difficulties came to them, and they grew afraid. The prospect of visiting a barbarous, fierce and pagan nation, whose language they did not speak and whose reputation for cruelty and savagery had spread throughout Europe, appalled them. They consulted together and it was agreed that Augustine himself should return to Rome and appeal to Pope Gregory to relieve them of the terrible duty he had laid upon them.

Augustine retraced his steps and saw Gregory, but the latter remained firm, giving Augustine fresh instructions in a letter which is dated 23rd July 596, and which Augustine was to carry back to his anxious companions. In the letter Gregory told the mission that it would have been better never to have taken up the task than to abandon it once it had begun. He insisted that, with God's help, they must fulfil their duty. Moreover he formally appointed Augustine as abbot of the party, possibly to give him fuller authority and to ensure greater obedience to him in future. All this suggests that Augustine himself may have been anxious to proceed, but had been faced with an almost direct refusal on the part of other and more faint-hearted members of the mission. Gregory's letter ended on a personal note. His office, he wrote, prevented him from working side by side with the mission, though he had always wished to do so. Here again we catch a glimpse of the lasting impression made upon him by his meeting with the young Angles in Rome.

Gregory also gave Augustine a letter to Etherius, Bishop of Lyons. (Bede in his account wrongly describes Etherius as Bishop of Arles.) This document was a formal letter of introduction and requested Etherius to give Augustine and his party all help, both spiritual and material. It also informed the bishop that Augustine would explain to him the purpose of the mission. The letter bears the same date as the first one addressed to the mission itself. These documents help us to see Augustine earnestly discussing his difficulties with Gregory during the hot days of that Roman summer. For his expedition to succeed he needed three things: full authority over the wavering and fearful members of his party, the Pope's direct exhortation to them, and the support of bishops on the way, so that his men could pause on their journey to gain new strength from congenial surroundings and a few days of tranquillity. And we can see Gregory, anxious for the success of the endeavour that lay so close to his heart, calling for a secretary and dictating, in some cool and shady room, the two letters that Augustine was to carry.

Armed with his new authority as abbot, Augustine hastened back to where his unwilling and apprehensive companions awaited him. He told them the result of his meeting with the Pope, showed them the letter and led them northwards across Gaul.

After spending some time with Etherius at Lyons, they resumed their journey to the sea. We do not know from which port they sailed. But we know that, by an extraordinary coincidence, Augustine and his companions came ashore on the small island of Thanet off the coast of Kent, the very place where Hengist and his Saxon troops had been settled a hundred and fifty years before. This was the place where the event had taken place that led to the destruction of Christianity over wide areas of the island; and this was the place where the rebuilding was to begin. The party that landed now included all of forty men. For Augustine had increased his numbers by bringing out of Gaul several Franks who spoke Latin and could serve as his interpreters with the English.

From Thanet they sent a message to King Aethilberht, to say that they had come from Rome bringing good news. This was, that all who would follow the doctrine that they were teaching would enjoy an eternal kingdom in heaven with the true and living God.

Aethilberht had become one of the most powerful kings in the island. He had extended his rule far beyond the confines of the Kentish promontory from which his kingdom took its name; he now ruled all the lands northwards to the River Humber. His wide dominions were matched by the pride of his ancestry, for he was the great-great-grandson of Hengist. He sent back a cautious but friendly reply, ordering the missionaries to remain within the Isle of Thanet, where they would be looked after, until he decided what action to take. The king was in any case predisposed to welcome them. For, as we have seen and as Augustine himself must have learned when he was in Gaul, his queen was Bertha, a Christian princess from the kingdom of the Franks.

Augustine and his party were not kept waiting long. Within a few days Aethilberht had made his decision and went to the Isle of Thanet to visit them. A chair was set for him in the open air, and there, with his nobles and attendants around him, he sent for Augustine to meet him under the trees and the late summer sky. It may have been superstition that prompted the king. He knew that his visitors were priests, and this meant that they might have powers of witchcraft. These powers, as all men knew, could be exercised in a house, but not in open fields in the light of day. Augustine and his company came in full procession, as if they wished to show that they could match the earthly splendour of the king. At their head marched a monk carrying a great silver cross that served as their ensign. Another bore a portrait of Christ painted on a panel. And as they came they offered up a prayer and sang a litany for the salvation of the king's people.

The king invited them to be seated and then told them of his decision. He himself could not forsake the ancient faith of the English people. But, since they had journeyed so far in order to teach what they sincerely believed to be right and good, he would not hinder them in their work. He would therefore supply them with whatever they needed and gave them permission to teach their religion to the people and to receive into their faith such of the king's people as wished to follow the new belief. Moreover he said that he would give them lodgings in his own royal town of Canterbury, the capital of his kingdom. They marched to the city in formal and solemn procession, with silver cross and painted portrait, chanting their prayers for the safety of the king's capital and for the house which he had given them.

After a short while the king granted them a further privilege. We have seen how Queen Bertha had restored for her use an ancient church. This church, which lay in the eastern party of the city, had been dedicated to St Martin of Tours, and the king allowed Augustine and his party to worship there. Here they prayed, here they celebrated Mass, here they taught the people and here they baptized their converts. So the beginnings of the Church in England lay in a building erected by the Christians of Roman Britain many centuries before the coming of Augustine.

At first the royal permission was a limited one, for the missionaries were allowed to teach only in this one church. However, it was not long before the king himself, impressed by the dedication and unselfishness of his guests from Rome, as well as by their promises of immortality, accepted Christianity and was baptized. Once this was known, people flocked in great numbers to hear the missionaries. The king gave them permission to preach wherever they wished, to build new churches and to restore the old Romano-British churches that stood deserted and derelict after long years of neglect. Moreover he endowed the fellowship with property in Canterbury, thus ensuring that they wanted for nothing.

Although many of his subjects followed the king's example, he was at pains not to use his royal authority to compel anyone to adopt the new religion. On the other hand he is reported as having shown especial favour to those of his subjects who followed his example.

Now that his mission had achieved success, with Christianity growing apace in the lands of the English, Augustine travelled to Arles to visit Archbishop Vergilius. The latter, on Pope Gregory's instructions, consecrated Augustine archbishop of the English people. On his return to Britain Augustine wrote a long letter to Gregory asking advice on many matters concerning his new duties as archbishop. His questions and Gregory's replies have been preserved.

Augustine had noticed in his travels across Europe that Christian customs and observances varied from place to place. For example, the manner of celebrating Mass in the churches of Gaul was different from that in Rome. One of his questions to Gregory, therefore, was how this had come about. The Pope's reply is an interesting one. Without explaining the reasons for these divergencies, he told Augustine that from all the customs which he had observed within the Roman or the Gaulish churches, he should make a careful selection; he should teach to the Church of the English whatever he felt could profitably be taken from any of the other churches. There is something almost prophetic in the fact that the infant Church of the English was so early exhorted to follow a policy of compromise in liturgy and in doctrine, since the independent Church of England was later to be founded upon just that principle.

Also prophetic was another of Augustine's questions, for it was clearly asked on behalf of King Aethilberht, in order to assist the latter in framing laws for his kingdom. A thousand years later the Church of England took the King of England as its head. Here, at its very birth, the new Church in England was helping an English king in the task of government. Moreover the king was issuing laws to protect the Church, and supporting the ecclesiastical establishment with his royal power. For the question asked by Augustine was: What punishments ought to be given to people who robbed churches? The Pope's answer was that the punishment should vary with the offence, a fine, a flogging or something even more severe. Aethilberht's laws have been preserved in a copy made in the early twelfth century. Characteristic of laws of the Anglo-Saxon kings in this sense, they lay down various fines for various offences. The first of the laws defines the scale of fines for the theft of ecclesiastical property. The fines were to be

The Hinton St Mary mosaic, with the portrait believed to be of Christ (centre of lower panel)

Restoration of second-century wall painting, Lullingstone Villa

twelve times the value of the stolen goods if they belonged to the church itself, elevenfold for a bishop's property, ninefold for a priest's, a deacon's sixfold and a clerk's threeefold.[1] There is no mention of the flogging recommended by Gregory! This law indicates how quickly Christianity had spread in Aethilberht's dominions, for only a large number of churches, possessing valuable property, would have justified such a special law.

There were numerous other points upon which Augustine sought guidance. One in particular contained the seeds of important events. What, asked Augustine, was to be his relationship with the bishops of Gaul and of Britain? He did not limit the scope of his question to the kingdom of Kent in which his mission was working, but to the whole of Britain. By now he would have heard of the island's ancient Christian traditions and of the churches of the Britons that lay in the west. His question implied that he saw his primacy as possibly giving him a special authority over all of them. Gregory's reply confirmed that this was so, for he told Augustine that he was to have charge of all the bishops in Britain. As to Gaul, Gregory was very definite. Augustine was to have no authority there whatsoever. When visiting Gaul he could inspire by example and give encouragement and advice. But that was all. The field of Gaul belonged to the Archbishop of Arles and Augustine was not to reap another's harvest. But there was no such thought for the feelings of the bishops of Britain. All (and this phrase by implication included all the bishops among the ancient Christian community of the Britons) came under Augustine's charge. The new ecclesiastical Rome was renewing the authority of the old military Rome, and bringing the old province back into the lands it governed.

But Britain had been independent of Rome for too long for her to accept easily this renewal of outside authority. The Britons resented the calm assumption of power by a stranger. They were proud of the Church which they themselves had built over the centuries and proud of their own ancient organization. They could not see why they should now submit themselves to the rule of a foreigner and of one who had identified himself with the English, setting up his see and his churches in lands that had been theirs, and of which they had been bloodily despoiled by the very people who now harboured him.

[1] R. W. Chambers, op. cit.

The ancient Church of the Britons and the infant Church of the English were to come into bitter conflict. The two nations were to resume, in affairs of religion, the struggle they had waged for so long on the battlefield. And the outcome was to be the same. For it was the new English Church that was to triumph.

8

THE TWO CHURCHES

WE DO not know by what means news travelled through Britain in those days, nor how it crossed the frontier lands of river and forest that divided the two hostile nations of the Britons and the English. But tidings of such a notable event as the conversion of Aethilberht, one of the most powerful of the English kings, must soon have come to the Britons in their diminished kingdoms in the west. There, in spite of military defeat and disaster, churches and monasteries were still flourishing; many of the latter had become well established and complex societies. The monastery at Bangor, for example, is said to have housed over two thousand monks. The community did not depend upon alms, but was a self-supporting fellowship, the monks living by the labour of their own hands. Throughout the regions occupied by the Britons the apostolic succession of priests and bishops had continued unbroken since the earliest time. The people lacked neither devotion to the faith nor wise leaders to guide them.

With what emotions they received the news that their hereditary enemies the English were now joining the Christian community we do not know. No records survive on their side, and the story has to be drawn from English sources. But the Britons seem to have heard the news with no rejoicing, nor did they see the events in Kent as the end of their long struggle with the English. Perhaps their ancient enmity and unrelenting bitterness against the ravagers of their land held them back, or perhaps their society had, after so many decades of isolation, grown solitary and almost morbidly inward looking; the fact is that they made no move to approach the new Christian community that was developing in the south-east of the island. The initiative for the first contact was made by Augustine.

Armed with the written authority which the Pope had given him 'over all the bishops in Britain', he obtained Aethilberht's permission to invite for a discussion the bishops and other most learned men from the nearest territory of the Britons. The kingdom of Kent had no common frontier with any land where the Britons dwelt, and the meeting therefore took place on the western borders of Wessex at a place called Augustine's Oak. There the British bishops came, no doubt filled with wary curiosity, eyeing the strange visitors cautiously and guardedly. Augustine addressed them and made an immediate appeal for Christian unity within the island. He asked the Britons to help him to establish full relations between the two Churches; more important, he urgently invited them to join him and his companions in the task of preaching the gospel far and wide to the heathen population of the English kingdoms. Though these proposals meant that the old province would again become a Christian island, sullenly and stubbornly the Britons refused both requests.

As to Christian unity, the main issue that divided them from Augustine seems to modern minds a trivial one. The Britons were still calculating the date of Easter in accordance with the edict of 455, for after that date communications between them and Gaul had broken down and news of the modified method of calculating Easter, adopted throughout the Christian world, had not reached them. Augustine therefore proposed that they should now bring their customs into line with those of all other Christian Churches. But the Britons would not yield, and stubbornly answered that they could not forsake their own long-established practices. They clearly resented this interference in their affairs, and the discussion seems to have been a stormy one, with an exasperated Augustine vainly trying every form of argument, advice and cajolery. On the Britons' reaction to the proposal for a joint mission to the English, the record of this first conference is silent. But it is clear from later events that this too was rejected. Finally, to prove to the stubborn Britons that he spoke with the full authority of heaven, Augustine is said to have performed a miracle of healing upon a blind Englishman. The Britons were sufficiently impressed to say that they would again consider his proposals after they had consulted with their own people.

It was accordingly agreed that the conference should be adjourned. Seven British bishops were appointed to attend the second session, together with various other learned men. Most of these came from the great monastery at Bangor, and they were carefully selected by their abbot, Dinoot.

The Britons discussed with one another at length whether it would be right for them to abandon their ancient traditions, to please this foreign bishop who had made new converts among their hereditary enemies. To many of them it appeared utterly unreasonable to do so. Their own Christian community had a history of many hundred years, and pride in its high achievements stiffened them in their resolve. Moreover Augustine, too confident of his authority and perhaps a trifle imperious, had failed to convince them that he was the right man to follow. So the Britons discussed their dilemma, and one of the men they consulted was a hermit. He said that they should first satisfy themselves that Augustine was indeed a man of God. When they asked him how they might do this he said: 'Our Lord says "take my yoke upon you and learn of Me for I am meek and lowly of heart". Therefore if Augustine is meek and lowly of heart, it will show that it is indeed the yoke of Christ that he bears, and that it is this yoke that he offers you.' But if he showed the sin of pride, then they should not accept him. Augustine's demeanour at the first conference had not been such that the British bishops could assure the hermit that they had found him a humble man! His arguments had been too masterful and his manner too overbearing. How could they be sure?

The hermit devised a simple test. The Britons should go to the conference a few minutes late so that Augustine and his companions would already be seated. If on their entry he courteously rose, this would be a sufficient sign of humility and they could accept him as a true emissary of Christ the humble. But if he remained seated, they should take this as a sign of pride and reject him, declining either to follow him or to change their ancient customs.

The plan was carried out. And Augustine remained seated.

Thus vanished any slender hope there might have been that the two Churches, British and English, could work together. So the conference began, with the resentful Britons smarting under the foreigner's discourtesy, reinforced in their views. Again the discussion was a stormy one: the Britons upbraided Augustine for his pride and angrily contradicted all that he said. He finally proposed a compromise. He would yield on all minor points of doctrine and practice that separated them, provided they on their side would agree to three things: first, they should celebrate Easter at the same time as all other Churches; next, they should administer the sacrament of baptism in accordance with the rites of the Roman Church; finally, they should join with the new Church in Kent in organizing a mission to all the English peoples. But the seven British bishops were in no mood for compromise. Out of hand they rejected Augustine's proposals. They did so not because of the merits or demerits of the three points; they argued that his discourtesy in not rising to greet them showed how little respect he had for them, and how little they could expect once they placed themselves under his authority and accepted him as archbishop over the whole island. For this reason alone they insisted vehemently that they would retain their independence at all costs, and continue along the road which they and their predecessors had been travelling for so long.

The sin of pride was obviously present on both sides. Augustine's pride seems to have been grounded in his own office and authority, and perhaps in his own ability. It is significant that Gregory found it necessary to write to him on one occasion warning him against the sin of boastfulness. The pride of the Britons, on the other hand, was not in their personal qualities or in the offices they held, but in the long and honourable history of the Church they represented. They could see no reason to yield their authority to an intruder from Rome and, through him, to their ancient enemies the English, with whom he was so closely identified. Throughout the lands of Europe the bishops of Rome had inherited something of the authority of the emperors, but this was not so in Britain. Isolated as they had been from developments on the Continent, for the Britons Rome had now become an empty name and Augustine therefore advanced in vain the authority which he had received from Pope Gregory, Bishop of Rome.

Before the meeting broke up Augustine had one last word to say. He told the Britons that if they refused to join with him they would be attacked and punished by their English enemies. We do not know whether this was a prophecy of divine retribution or an earthly threat. But to the Britons, because Augustine was working so closely with

King Aethilberht, in whose name they had been summoned to the conference, the words must have sounded like open menace and yet another example of his arrogance. Prophecy or threat, it was to be terribly fulfilled. In the meantime the conference ended and broke up in disagreement. Augustine, frustrated in his purpose, returned to Kent and the Britons departed to their own land.

The hopes of unity faded. Augustine's plan of a British Church, with himself as archbishop wielding authority over all the bishops and priests in the lands of the old province—Briton, English and Roman alike—was not to be fulfilled. The Britons withdrew into renewed isolation. The conflict between the two nations, which might have been brought to an end by a common religion and a common purpose, continued. The identities of the two peoples gradually changed. The independent Britons became a new nation, the Welsh; and the scattered tribes and kingdoms of Angles, Saxons and Jutes, together with Britons still dwelling among them, became the English people. War between them was to continue for many centuries, and the peace which might have been made at Augustine's Oak was long postponed.

Some time after the fruitless meeting of the Britons with Augustine the wars against them were renewed. In Northumbria the English were still pagan and were ruled by King Aethilfrid, a great military leader. He gathered together an army and attacked the Britons near the old Roman city of Chester, once the garrison town of the Twentieth Legion.

With the army of the Britons there marched twelve hundred and fifty of the monks from Bangor, to pray for the victory of the Christian soldiery over the heathen host of the English. On the day of battle these stood a little apart from the armies. A Briton named Brocmail with a small detachment mounted guard over them.

When King Aethilfrid was told of this he said: 'If these men invoke their God against me, then they are fighting against us, even though they bear no arms!' And he ordered his troops to attack them. Brocmail, at the first onset, was put to flight, and the English slaughtered the unarmed monks, of whom only fifty escaped with their lives. The menacing words of Augustine had come true. The blood of the monks of Bangor was the terrible outcome of the meeting at Augustine's Oak.[1]

[1] The material for this chapter is drawn from Bede's *Ecclesiastical History*.

The defeated Britons long remembered the bloody day and recorded it as the battle 'in which the saints were slain'.[1]

A river of blood again flowed between the English and the Britons. Because Augustine dwelt among the English he could never be accepted by the Britons. How could he be a true Christian who worked among those savage Englishmen? How could he hope to convert men who had butchered unarmed monks and whose hands were stained with the blood of the saints? This and other stories lingered long among them and among their kinsfolk, both bond and free, living in the English kingdoms. It may not be altogether fanciful to believe that their bitter memories may have coloured Christian thought in the island permanently and deeply. In later years, when peace was made between the two Churches, and when missionaries from the Celtic Church finally came among the English, it is not impossible that the latter too came to be influenced by the tales of old wrongs and ancient cruelties.

It was to be nearly a thousand years after the meeting at Augustine's Oak that the Church in England finally broke with Rome, refusing any longer to accept the special authority claimed by the Bishop of Rome, and taking their own king as head of their Church. Maybe in those events are to be heard the last faint echoes of those old sorrows, still persisting through ten centuries.

[1] Tigernach, *Annales*.

INDEX

Aaron, British martyr, 36
Abgar, Lucius Aelius Septimius, 19
Adamnan, Abbot of Iona, 85, 121
Adelphius, Bishop, (?) of Colchester, 43
Aelle, King, 130
Aethilberht, King, 123, 131 *et seq.*
Aethilfrid, King, 142
Aetius, consul, 101–2
Agricola, governor of Britain, 10, 35
Agricola, a Pelagian, 90
Ailred, 80, 81
Alban, St, 35
Albeus, Bishop of Munster, 116
Albinus, Abbot, 18
Allectus, murders Carausius, 33, 44
All-Hallows-by-the-Tower, 50
Amator, Bishop, 74, 93
Ambrose, St, 36
Ambrosius Aurelianus, 111–13
Ammianus, 100 *n.*
Ampleforth, Christian objects, 59
Andrew, St, 130; monastery of, 132
Anglo-Saxon Chronicle, 103, 104, 109
Annwn, ruler of Galloway, 79
Antoninus Pius, Emperor, 17, 24
Antonius, ruler of Galloway, 79, 80
Arles, Synod of, 41–4, 45; Council of Bishops at, 61; Augustine travels to, 136; Archbishop, 137
Armagh, 114
Armorica, 98, 119
Arthur, King, 113, 114
Asclepiodotus, Praetorian Prefect, 33
Athanasius, 44 *n.*
Athenagoras, 7
Augustine (of Canterbury), ix–x, 59, 84, 110, 132–43
Augustine (of Hippo), 85, 86, 88
Augustine's Oak, 139, 142
Augustus, policy to Britain, 3, 4
Aurelius, Marcus, Emperor, 17, 18, 19, 24; his *Meditations*, 25 *n.*
Auxerre, St Patrick at, 74, 85, 92

Babylas, St, 28
Badonicus (Badon), Mount, 111–12, 113, 118, 123
Bangor, 138, 140, 142
Bannavem Tabernae, 71
Barrovadus, erects memorial stone in Galloway, 82
Bedd Gwyl Illtyd, 99
Bede, ix *n.*; on King Lucius, 18; on the building of the church at St Albans, 41; on Ninian, 79, 81; on the Pelagians, 90 *n.*, 91 *n.*, 94 *n.*; on St Germanus, 96; on Anglo-Saxon advance, 104 *n.*; on King Aethilfrid, 123 *n.*; on Anglo-Saxon gods, 125; on the British Church, 127; on Saxon slaves in Rome, 130 *n.*; on St Martin's Church, 131 *n.*; on Augustine's mission, 142 *n.*
Bellerophon, depictions of, 51–4
Bertha, Queen, ix, 131, 134, 135
Biconys, father of Iltudus, 98
Boudicca, 17
Boulogne, *see* Gessoriacum
Bridius, King, receives Columba, 120
Britio, 19
Britannia Prima, British province, 33
Britannia Secunda, British province, 33
Brocmail, a British warrior, 142

Cadoc, St, 98
Caecilian, 42
Caecina Severus, 9
Caerleon-on-Usk, Aaron and Julius martyred at, 36; 38, 117, 118
Caesar, Julius, plans conquest of Britain, 3, 129
Caesarea, Christians destroy Temple of Fortune at, 62
Caledonia, 76
Caligula, Emperor, fails to invade Britain, 5; puts to death Julius Graecinus, 10
Calixtus I, Pope, 19, 28 *n.*
Calixtus II, Pope, 119
Calleva Atrebatum, *see* Silchester

Calpurnius, father of St Patrick, 71, 72–3
Candida Casa, 81
Candidus, Gregory's letter to, 131
Canterbury, Roman Church at, ix; Christian objects from, 56; King Aethilberht's capital, 131; St Augustine at, 135
Canterbury Cathedral, 50
Cantii, 105, 123
Canwick, church at, 50
Caracalla, Emperor, 25, 27–9
Caradoc of Llancarfan, 109
Carausius, murdered by Allectus, 33; Britain's separation under, 44
Carthage, dispute over appointment of Bishop of, 86, 87
Cassius, C. Avidius, 19
Ceawlin, King of Wessex, 123
Celestine I, Pope, 75, 91 *n.*
Cerdic, King of Wessex, 123
Ceredig, father of Sanctus, 126
Chedworth, villa at, 58
Chester, headquarters of the Twentieth Legion, 38; 142
Chrysanthus, 66, 92
Cirencester, word square at, 11–14; inscribed stone at, 63, 104
Claudius, Emperor, conquest of Britain, ix, 5; praises Aulus Plautius, 6; expels Jews, 7; 17
Clemens, Flavius, 23
Clonard, Columba studies at, 120
Coel, possible 'Old King Cole', 37
Coelestius, 86, 91
Collingwood, R. G., 85 *n.*, 86 *n.*, 88
Columba, St, 85, 120–1
Columbanus, 85
Columella, 10 *n.*
Commodus, Emperor, 25
Conal Gulban, father of Columba, 120
Constans, Emperor, 60
Constantine the Great, Emperor, x, 36–44, 47, 60, 61
Constantine II, Emperor, 60
Constantinople, 60, 87, 129, 130
Constantius, priest of Lyons, 92
Constantius, Emperor, Caesar under Maximian, 33; 37, 41, 43
Constantius II, Emperor, 60, 61, 62
Copthall Court, bowl from, 57
Corinium, *see* Cirencester
Cornelius, Pope, 29
Cothrige, a name of St Patrick, 73
Cuminius, Abbot of Iona, 121
Cunedda, grandfather of Sanctus, 116
Cunobelin, King, 3, 4, 5
Cyprian, St, 29
Cyril, St, of Jerusalem, 37

Dalaradis, 73
Damasus, Pope, 77
David, St, at Glastonbury, 15; his life, 117–19
Decius, Emperor, 23, 27
Deira, kingdom of, 124, 130
Denys (of Alexandria), 28
Denys (the Aeropagite), 16
Derry, monastery of, 120
Dichu, 75, 76
Diocletian, Emperor, 18; government, 33; and the Christians, 34; 38, 41
Diospolis, 87
Domitian, Emperor, 23
Domitilla, 23
Donatus, Bishop, 42
Drepanum, birthplace of Helena, 36
Dura-Europos, 13
Durovernum, *see* Canterbury
Durrow, 120
Dyfan, 18 *n.*
Dyfrig, St, 117, 119

Eborius, (?) Bishop of York, 43
Elagabalus, Emperor, 27–9
Eleutherius, Pope, 6, 18, 19
Elfan, 18 *n.*
Elvira, Synod of, 34, 71 *n.*
Etherius, Bishop of Lyons, 133
Eucharisto, Pope, 18
Eusebius, 24; describes conditions under Commodus, 25; on Church under Caracalla, 26 *n.*; on Julia Mammaea, 28 *n.*; on Decius, 29;

on Diocletian, 34; on Helena, 37; on the vision of Constantine, 39, 40; on the Edict of Milan, 42
Eusebius, Bishop of Nicomedia, 60
Eutropius, 36
Evaristo, Pope, 19

Fabian, Pope, 29
Fastidius, British writer, 88–90
Fatalis, 88
Ffagan, 18 *n.*
Finian, St, 120
Flavia Caesariensis, province of Britain, 33
Florentius, 84
Frampton, Christian villa at, 51

Galerius, Caesar, 33; 34, 36, 37
Gallienus, Emperor, 29
Galloway, 79, 80
Garton, Donegal, 120
Gaul, 3; trade between Britain and, 4; Christian visitors to Britain from, 6; 33; Constantine establishes his headquarters in, 39; ruled by Constantine II, 60; the bishops of, 91; 93, 128; Augustine journeys through, 133–4; 136
Gennadius, 88–9
Germanilla, mother of St Germanus, 92
Germanus, St, Bishop of Auxerre, 74; missions to Britain, 87; his activities in Britain, 90–8; 99; Paulinus a pupil of, 117
Gessoriacum, base of Aulus Plautius, 5; Constantius invades Britain from, 37; Constantine at, 38
Gibbon, Edward, 8, 24, 34
Gildas, 6 *n.*; 35, 45, 98, 109–15, 118, 119, 123, 126–7, 129
Giraldus Cambrensis, 16, 117 *n.*
Glabrio, M. Acilius, 23
Glasnevin, 120
Glastonbury, 6; legend, 14–17; 114
Glevum, *see* Gloucester
Gloucester, 104, 105
Gordian, Emperor, 28
Goths, Rome sacked by, 80
Graecinus, Julius, father of Agricola, 10
Gratian, Emperor, 65
Gregory, Pope, x, 130–3, 136–7, 141

Hadrian, Emperor, 17, 24
Helena, mother of Constantine, x, 36
Helenopolis, named after Helena, 36
Hengist, invited by Vortigern, 102; death of, 113, 122; succeeded by Aesc, 123; 134
Hen Mynw, *see* Old Menevia
Hibernia, 75
Hill of Slane, 76
Hippolytus, St, 28
Hipponoüs, original name of Bellerophon, 52
Historia Augusta, 17 *n.*, 27 *n.*
Holy Grail, 16
Honorius, Emperor, 87, 90
Hueil, brother of Gildas, 114

Icklingham, 'font' from, 58
Ida, King, 123
Ides, buried in Galloway, 84
Illtyd, St, 98, 119
Iltudus, *see* Illtyd
Imigonus, a name of St Patrick, 72
Innespatrick, 75
Innocent I, Pope, 87
Iona, 120–1
Irenaeus, St, his list of Christian lands, 6
Isca, *see* Exeter

Jerome, St, 80
Jews, expelled from Rome, 7; their religious propaganda banned, 26
John, Bishop of Jerusalem, 86
John, St, 15
Joseph of Arimathaea, 6, 14–17
Josephus, 10 *n.*
Julia, daughter of Drusus, 7, 8, 10
Julia Domna, wife of Commodus, 25, 27 *n.*
Julia Maesa, 25

Julia Mammaea, 25, 27
Julian, Emperor, 'The Apostate', 27 *n.*, 61–3, 64
Julian of Aeclanum, 87
Julian, Prefect, 93
Julius, British martyr, 36
Julius Africanus, visits Rome, 28
Justin, martyr, 24

Kent, ix–xi, 47, 50, 55, 59, 102, 103, 104, 122, 123, 134 *et seq.*
Kirkmadrine, inscribed stones at, 83

Lactantius, 34, 39, 42 *n.*
Laoghaire, High King of Ireland, 75, 76
Latinus, buried in Galloway, 82
Laurentius, priest, 132
Leo, Pope, 128
Lerins, monastery of, 74
Licinius, Emperor, signs the Edict of Milan, 42; shares power with Constantine, 44
Liudhard, Bishop, 131
Llancarfan, 98, 114
Llandewi-Brefi, 117-18
Llandaff, church of, 18 *n.*, 119
Lleur Mawr, 18 *n.*
Loco Tegiacum, monastery of St Martin, 77
Loco Teiac, 77, 81
London, 4; Constantius arrives at, 33; mint at, 60; name changed, 78; Britons retreat into, 102
Lucius, King, 6, 15 *n.*, 17–19
Luke, St, 15
Lupus, Bishop of Troyes, 93–4
Lyminge, church at, 50
Lullingstone, room used for Christian worship in villa at, 47–9, 51, 52
Lyons, Bishopric of, 5; persecution at, 25; 92, 133

Macrianus, Praetorian Prefect, 29
Macrinus, 27–9
Magloconus, 98, 119
Magnentius, Emperor, 55
Magonus, a name of St Patrick, 72
Marcia, concubine of Commodus, 25
Margate, Christian lamp from, 57
Mark, St, 14
Martin, St, ix; visited by St Ninian, 77; 131, 135
Matthew, St, 15
Mavorius, buried in Galloway, 84
Maxentius, son of Maximian, 39
Maxima Caesariensis, a province of Britain, 33
Maximian, Emperor, 34, 36, 39
Maximin, Emperor, 27–9
Maximus, Emperor, 64, 65, 71, 77
Maximus, P. Anicius, 10
Maxin Wledig, 79
Medwy, 18 *n.*
Menevia, *see* Old Menevia
Milan, Edict of, 41–4; council, 61
Milchu, 73, 74, 75
Mildenhall, silver objects from, 57
Milvian Bridge, Constantine's victory at, 39
Mynyw, *see* Old Menevia

Namatius, 99
Nau, King of Scotia, 109
Nennius, 18 *n.*, 112, 113, 118 *et seq.*
Nero, Emperor, 7, 10, 23
Nestorius, 27
Niall, King of the Nine Hostages, 120
Nicaea, Council of, 44; 87
Nicomedia, 34, 36, 37, 38, 60
Ninian, St, 77–84, 127
Non, mother of Sanctus, 116
Nothelm, a priest from London, 18
Novantae, 80

Octavian, *see* Augustus
Offa, King, founds monastery in St Albans, 35
Oghgul (Angles), 124
Old Menevia, 116, 118
Origen, 3, 5, 28
Orosius, 36, 86, 101
Osroëne, a Roman dependency, 19

Palladius, a deacon, 75, 91 *n.*

Pannonia, 10; ruled by Constans, 60
Patrick, St (his life), 71–6; 98, 112, 120, 127
Paul, St, 115
Paulinus, Milanese deacon, 86
Paulinus, St, 117
Paulinus, Suetonius, governor of Britain, 17
Pelagians, 90–8
Pelagius, 85–7, 117
Pelagius II, Pope, 130–1
Penda, King, 124–5
Peter, monk, 132
Peter, St, 83
Philip (the Apostle), 15
Philip, Emperor (the Arabian), 27
Philostratus, 27 *n.*
Picts, Constantine defeats, 38; driven out by Julian, 64; 66, 77, 78, 79, 92, 94, 96–7, 100, 101, 102, 120
Plautius, Aulus, in command of invasion of Britain, 5; returns to Rome, 6–7; retires, 10
Pliny, the younger, 24
Pompeii, 13
Pomponia Graecina, whether a Christian, 6–11
Pontian, 29
Pothrige, a name of St Patrick, 73
Potitus, 71
Prittlewell, Essex, church, 49
Procilla, Julia, wife of Julius Graecinus, 10
Procopius, 129
Ptolemy, the geographer, 79

Raphaneae, 10
Ratae, *see* Leicester
Restitutus, Bishop of London, 43
Rhygyvarch, 117 *n.*
Richborough, Roman army lands at, 5; Constantius lands at, 33, 38
Rimini, Council of, 44, 61
Rusticus, father of St Germanus, 92

St Albans, 36; mosaic at, 47; cathedral built of Roman bricks, 50; St Germanus at, 95
St Bride's Church, London, part composed of Roman materials, 50
St David's, 118, 119
St Peter's Church, Rome, 131
Sanctus, father of St David, 116
Sandde, *see* Sanctus
Sardica, Council of, 44
Saul, Church of, 75, 76
Saxa Rubra, Constantine's victory at, 39
Saxons, 64, 94, 96, 97, 100, 102, 103, 104, 110, 111, 122 *et seq.*
Scots, driven out by Julian, 64; attack the Roman provinces, 66; taught by Columba, 120; 127
Selgovae, 80
Senicianus, recipient of a Christian ring, 56
Septimius, L., 63
Severianus, father of Agricola the Pelagian, 90
Severus, Alexander, Emperor, 27–9
Severus, Flavius, 37
Severus, Septimius, Emperor, dies at York, 17; public acts against the Christians, 26
Sidonius Appollinaris, letter from on the subject of the Saxons, 99
Silchester, 10; (?) church at, 45–7
Siricius, Pope, 77
Sol Invictus, on Constantine's coins, 40
Southwell Minster, 50
Spain, 3; ruled by Constantine II, 60
Stansted Mountfichet, church, 50
Stilicho, 66
Strabo, on Britain, 4
Strangford Lough, 75, 120
Succat, first name of St Patrick, 72
Suetonius, 7, 8
Syagrius, 58

Tacitus, 7, 8, 9, 10, 11, 17 *n.*, 100 *n.*
Tara, 76
Teilo, 119
Tertullian, on Christianity in Britain, 6; on Caracalla, 25; on Septimius Severus, 26

Thanet, 102, 134
Theodosius, Count, 64; Emperor, 65, 66
Tiberius, Emperor, 5, 10
Tigernach, *Annales*, 143
Tiu, 103
Toynbee, Professor J. M. C., 43 *n.*; 50, 53, 59 *n.*
Trajan, Emperor, 17, 24
Triedd Ynis Pritein, 16
Tudwal, 80
Turpilanus, Petronius, 17

Valerian, Emperor, 29
Vartry, River, 75
Verulamium, 41, 50, 95
Verus, Emperor, 19
Vetus Menevia, *see* Old Menevia
Victory, Synod of, 118
Virgil, credits Augustus with intention to invade Britain, 3; inscription referring to, 52
Virgilius, Archbishop, 136
Viventius, buried in Galloway, 84
Vortigern, King, invites the Saxons, 102, 104, 110; grants lands to the Saxons, 132

Wall, Hadrian's, 34, 64, 92, 101
Wessex, 123, 124, 139
West Mersea, church at, 50
Whithorn, 82
Whitland, St David educated at, 117
Widford, Roman villa, 50

York, Septimius Severus dies at, 17, 25; Constantius rebuilds fortres; at, 37; Constantius dies at, 38s Christian community at, 43; 125

Zosimus, 36; 87

BERAM SAKLATVALA was born in Manchester in 1911. One of his main interests is Roman history, and in particular Roman Britain. He translated the poems of François Villon for the Everyman's Library edition, and is the author of a number of books of verse, and also of *Arthur, Last Champion of Roman Britain.*